The 113 Keys to Acting

Hugh O'Gorman

California State University-Long Beach

KENDALL/HUNT PUBLISHING COMPANY
4050 Westmark Drive   P.O. Box 1840   Dubuque, Iowa 52004-1840

2800

Cartoons on cover and interior by Joshua Breeding

Copyright © 2007 by Hugh O'Gorman

ISBN 13: 978-0-7575-3771-4
ISBN 10: 0-7575-3771-5

Kendall/Hunt Publishing Company has the exclusive rights to
reproduce this work, to prepare derivative works from this work,
to publicly distribute this work, to publicly perform this work
and to publicly display this work.

Printed in the United States of America
10 9 8 7 6 5 4 3 2 1

CONTENTS

In memory of
Hubert J. O'Gorman, my father

INTRODUCTION

"The Play's the thing wherein I'll
catch the conscience of the king…"

- WILLIAM SHAKESPEARE — *HAMLET*

Hello and Welcome to the art of acting!

You hold in your hands *The 113 Keys to Acting: an introduction to acting for non-majors*! If truth be told, you've held the keys to acting in your hands since you were a child. But we will get to that later on in the book. This is a workbook about the art of acting. It is intended for those students with very little experience in this field or none at all. It is designed for the non-theatre major who wants to explore the alluring and mysterious world of the actor. Yet, one of the first things you will quickly learn in turning these pages is that for quite some time now you yourself have already been acting in the most majestic and compelling pageant known to mankind - life. In fact you have already set foot on the largest of all stages and played a multitude of parts in the spectacle known as the world we live in.

ACTORS AS STORY TELLERS

This book will lay bare for you the mystery of arguably the oldest art form. As long as mankind has been in existence there have been actors. For as long as there has been storytelling, someone was needed to actually recount the story. Storytelling is what acting is all about. Actors *play* different roles to portray a *story*. Therefore actors are storytellers. To do so successfully actors must shed the social masks they wear in their personal lives, and they must *play* with the unbridled enthusiasm and imagination of children.

THE "113 BIBLE"

This workbook is a text that evolved out of what is affectionately known in the theater arts department at California State University Long Beach as the "113 Bible". It is a compellation of explanations, definitions, exercises, reflections, and admonitions from the *Theatre Arts 113 class: Introduction to Acting for Non-majors.* It has been compiled through the collective effort of the dozens of brave graduate acting students in the California Repertory Company, professional actors who after successful careers in the art and business of acting have returned to earn the Master of Fine Arts degree in their chosen field. Much wisdom is contained within these covers – or so we do believe!

Do read it thoroughly. Yet remember, no matter how good a textbook is, no matter how good your professor is,

 EXPERIENCE IS THE BEST TEACHER!

Get up off your duff and onto your feet as often as possible in class!

ACTING IS DOING

You can learn about acting from a book. You cannot, however, learn to act from a book. This is an important distinction. That said, what this workbook can do is shed light on and flesh out the experiences you have in the classroom. It will also provide context, definition, history and serve as a reference and journal for your own work and growth as an actor/artist/human being.

   The objective of this workbook is to help increase your awareness of the art of acting, the theatre and the world around you by supplementing your in class experience with context, vocabulary and background. It is the hope of your teacher and myself that you will come to love acting as we have.

Welcome to the world of professional human beings…

Welcome to the art of acting!

Hugh O'Gorman

Head of Acting
California State University Long Beach

PART

WORK ON SELF

I

CHAPTER

PASSION

1

> *"Nothing great has been and nothing great can be accomplished without passion."*
>
> - Georg Wilhelm Friedrich Hegel

PASSION

Without passion life passes you by. Passion is the eternal spirit of existence. In this course you will be asked to do a lot of things that may challenge your passions. I encourage you to run right into those challenges even if they scare you.

 PASSION IS THE FUEL OF LIFE!

To act *passionately* in front of your peers, or write *passionately* about how you interpret a theatrical production is a victory you may not have anticipated in signing up for this course. But both will be asked of you in this class.

THE DEATH OF "WHATEVER..."

The flip side of passion is "Whatever..."; "Whatever...." How many times have you said this? Hopefully, not many. If you haven't said it at all, I commend you! But more and more often, especially in certain areas of this country, one hears this word ring out loud and clear with apathy and lethargy. "Whatever..." is a sign of complacency and lack of passion.

"WHATEVER..." SIGNIFIES A LACK OF COMMITMENT.

Acting takes huge commitment. My colleague in the theatre department here at California State University Long Beach, Craig Fleming, says that it is our job as teachers to bring about the death of "Whatever...." I couldn't agree more. It will help you immensely if you work actively and daily to rid this malaise from your life.

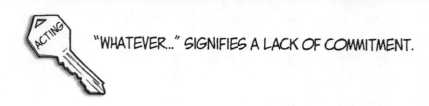 **HOW YOU TALK ABOUT YOUR WORK IS HOW YOUR WORK WILL BE!**

If you talk passionately about your work and your life, your actions in both with reflect it. Remember this. We will come back to it later.

THE DEATH OF "FLIP-FLOPS"

One cannot act passionately while wearing flip-flop shoes. It is impossible. If you wear them into your acting class, take them off and walk barefoot. Flip-flops are footwear designed for the "whatever..." crowd. They are fine for the beach and weekends, but not for taking action and leaning forward into life. In flip-flops you wait for life to come to you. Actors don't wait for life to come to them. They run head first into life.

 ACTORS NEED TO BE GROUNDED.

You cannot feel the ground beneath you if you are wearing flip-flops. So, get in touch with the ground under you and toss away those flip-flops for this class.

 FLIP-FLOPS ARE AN ONOMATOPOEIC SHOE FOR THE UNCOMMITTED!

EXERCISE

Answer the following questions:

Q Without thinking too much about it, what are your passions in life?

Q Do you consider yourself a passionate person? If so, why? If not, why not?

Q What areas of your life (i.e. work, personal relationships, school) could be improved upon if you became more passionate about them?

CHAPTER

> *"To live a creative life, we must lose our fear of being wrong."*
>
> - JOSEPH CHILTON PEARCE

GROWTH

Ideally, you enroll in a class in order to learn something new. Right? Perhaps you signed up for this class because your friend did, or because someone you have a crush on is taking it, or because you thought it might be an easy "A." Okay. These aren't terrible reasons. But they aren't inspiring ones, either. The truly unfortunate scenario would be the one in which you signed up for this class because you "had to." If this is indeed why you signed up then you definitely have to make a shift in your thinking, otherwise you probably won't get much out of this course, or any other for that matter.

But what if I were to suggest to you to look at the choice to take this class in a slightly different light?

 YOU SIGNED UP FOR THIS CLASS IN ORDER TO GROW AS A HUMAN BEING.

If you accept the premise that acting is about being a "professional human being," we can then assume that you are here to *grow* as a human being. Right?

 GROWTH HAPPENS WHERE YOU PUT YOUR ATTENTION.

It's that simple. Yet, as with all simple things, you must not take this for granted. Growth implies change. And most people are resistant to change on some level. In fact, you've surely heard the adage "You can't teach an old dog a new trick." Do you agree with this? Where do you think this saying came from? Is it that as we get older we become more resistant to change? This may be true for the average person. But it doesn't have to be. And it certainly cannot be true for the artist. As soon as an artist resists growth and change, their work dies. Artists are like sharks in that respect, they have to keep moving forward and changing direction to stay alive.

AN OPEN MIND

An open mind is essential to learning and growing. You will need to make yourself available to personal change in this class. There is no growth if there is no willingness to hear something new and possibly change. And unlike a lecture class in another subject, YOU are the material that we work with in acting. During the class your teacher may point out habits that you have when you do an exercise. You need to keep an open mind about their feedback. You should attempt to keep yourself open mentally, physically, vocally, and emotionally. It will be essential to your growth in this work.

CREATIVITY AND GROWTH

Creativity, by definition, requires giving birth to something new, something that hadn't existed before it was created. So, if you aren't willing and available to new possibilities then the chances are that you won't create anything.

SELF-DEFENSIVENESS

Self-defensiveness has no place in the acting studio. If you plan to stand in the corner with your arms crossed making fun of others in the class, I suggest you drop the class now. Self-defensiveness and a closed-off, negative energy is a sign of fear and weakness. Did you know one of the first things New York City police officers are taught when they join the academy? They are instructed never to cross their arms across their chest. Can you guess why? It is a sign of weakness. True strength comes from openness and availability—not closing yourself off. Keep this in mind as you move through this class. Try to let go of any self-defensive posturing that you may be initially inclined toward. Eventually, as you gain confidence, it will get easier and easier to remain open. This is when the real growth will happen for you.

EXERCISE

Answer the following questions:

Fear is the biggest thing that cripples us and keeps us from growing as artists and human beings. Growth requires doing things we are uncomfortable and even unfamiliar with.

Q Identify and list at least three fears that keep you from growing.

Q Can you identify the respective origins of these fears? Are they grounded in truth or have you simply come to accept them as truth?

Q What action can you take to eliminate those fears in order to grow?

Q Use the space below to log your progress in eradicating the fears you have identified.

EXERCISE EXERCISE EXERCISE EXERCISE EXERCISE EXERCISE EXERCISE

CHAPTER

CURIOSITY

3

> *"Every age has a keyhole
> to which its eye is pasted."*
>
> — MARY MCCARTHY

CURIOSITY

Remember the saying "Curiosity kills the cat?" Well, curiosity may be a uniquely feline pitfall, but for us humans it's the lifeblood to creativity. The inspiring voice teacher Catherine Fitzmaurice once said to me:

 CURIOSITY IS DESIRE OF THE MIND.

I have never forgotten these words and couldn't agree more. In order to get the most out of this class, or any other, you will have to be or become deeply curious about the subject matter as well as the world around you. What you take away from this course will have more to do with *your own curiosity* about acting than any other combination of singular or concerted factors.

 CURIOSITY IS THE GLUE THAT BINDS YOUR ATTENTION TO YOUR TARGET.

No less than the meta-genius Leonardo da Vinci said that curiosity was the first step in the acquisition of any knowledge or skill, craft, technique, or art. Without curiosity, the mind is feeble and easily distracted. Da Vinci dissected actual human bodies to perfect his drawing of the anatomy.

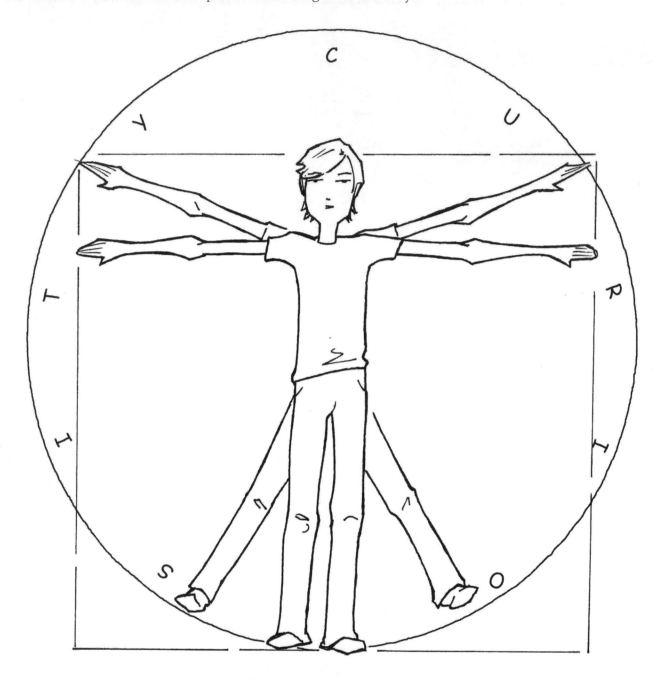

If you accept the premise that actors are professional human beings, then it goes without saying that to be an actor you will need to be curious about humanity.

EXERCISE

Answer the following questions:

Q Why are you curious about acting?

Q What other academic subjects are you curious about? Why?

Q What peaks your curiosity about your life in general? Why?

Exercise TO DO: To test your curiosity, over the next week find someone with whom you are already familiar and ask yourself, "Can I find three new physical traits about this person that hadn't noticed before?" List them below.

Exercise TO DO: This week become curious about two people in this class, and, without telling them, discover three new things about these people. List them below.

CHAPTER
OBJECTIVES FOR THIS CLASS
4

> *"The object of education is
> not to know—but to live!"*
>
> - Anonymous

CLASS OBJECTIVES

So, you signed up for introduction to acting. This may be your first acting class. Or maybe you were the star of your drama club in high school. It doesn't matter how much acting experience you have at this point. What does matter is why you are here now and what you want to get out of this class.

Have you given this serious thought? Do you know exactly why you are here right now?

CONSCIOUS PRESENCE IN THE HERE AND NOW IS AN ESSENTIAL KEY TO ACTING.

So, why are you here? Have you given this any thought?

Right now, without thinking about it, grab something to write with and start DOING.

ACTING IS DOING.

So, let's start doing…let's deal with *doing* something in the *here and now*. In the box below list the reasons why you signed up for this class. Then, also, list your personal goals for this class.

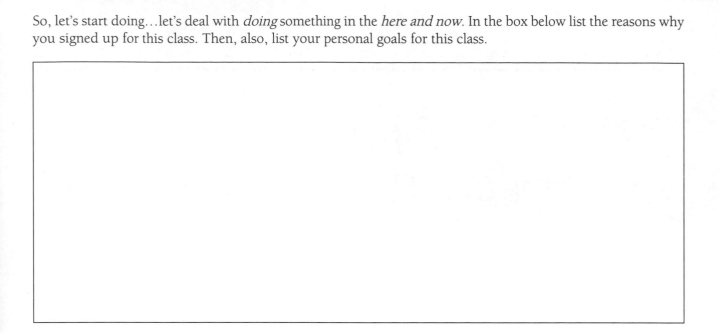

OBJECTIVE OBSERVATION OF SELF

So, did you know what your goals were? Did you know immediately? Or did you have to think about it for a while? It doesn't matter. Neither one is right or wrong. What is important is that you objectively note which was true for you.

OBJECTIVE OBSERVATION OF SELF IS ONE OF THE KEYS TO NOT ONLY ACTING BUT REACHING YOUR GOALS IN LIFE.

What *matters* is that you wrote something down. What *matters* is that you *committed* pen or pencil to paper and left a mark as to what you want. This is the beginning. If you don't know what you want, you won't go anywhere in this class, or for that matter, in life.

OBJECTIVES

Taking action matters, and there are no actions without goals. We all have wants, needs, and desires that pull us through life. They are the motivations that fuel our daily lives with "doing." These wants or goals are called objectives.

Our lives are composed of a string of small objectives. These objectives motivate our actions in any given moment, hour, day, week, month, year, or longer period of our lives. Objectives determine our actions.

IN ACTING, GOALS ARE CALLED OBJECTIVES.

Remember this. It's extremely important for acting. We'll come back to it later.

EXERCISE

Answer the following questions:

Q Why did you decide to take this class?

Q What are you goals for this class? In other words, what do you hope to gain from taking this course?

CHAPTER 5

THE SUPER-OBJECTIVE

*"Better a little which is well done,
than a great deal imperfectly."*

- PLATO

THE ULTIMATE GOAL: THE SUPER-OBJECTIVE

All of us have hopes and dreams for our lives. These hopes and dreams are the things that get us out of bed in the morning. Our daily existence is driven by our hopes and dreams. Most of these hopes and dreams are ultimately motivated by any combination of money, power, knowledge, recognition, or sex. One could argue that all motives in life come down to either ambition or sex. Some people are driven by one or two of these things and some by all of them! We believe, ultimately, that these things will bring us happiness and satisfaction, which seems to be almost everyone's ultimate goal no matter where you live on the globe.

This ultimate goal in life is called a super-objective. It is the ultimate objective that determines all the other smaller objectives. In other words, the super-objective is the thing you want, or desire, or are working toward, all the time. Even as you deal with smaller objectives along the way, this super-objective never leaves or changes. Most of the time our smaller objectives line up one-by-one, like pearl beads in a necklace, to help us achieve our super-objective.

Perhaps right now your super-objective for the next few years is to earn your college degree. Or maybe it's to get straight "A" grades in all your classes so you can win entrance into law, business, or medical school. Perhaps your super-objective is to become an Olympic athlete, a journalist, a banker, or a veterinarian. Although super-objectives are often related to professions, they need not necessarily be.

Super-objectives can be personal in nature as well. Many people have as a super-objective to eventually find a partner and raise a family, or to seek recognition, fame, or glory.

Or super-objectives can be more emotional and intangible, like to "be happy" or "live a compassionate life" or "stay healthy." They can even be "to be powerful" or "to gain respect."

As you can see, super-objectives take many forms. Although they are archetypal in nature, they are shaped by each individual's particular hopes and dreams.

 SUPER-OBJECTIVES ARE OUR HOPES AND DREAMS. THEY ARE THE FUEL FOR THE ACTIONS WE TAKE IN OUR LIVES.

This holds true for acting as well. Each character in a piece of dramatic fiction has a super-objective. Actors have to specifically know their character's super-objective in order to successfully play their part. They must also, therefore, know the character's smaller objectives in each scene as well. This is no different for the actor in a play, film, or television show.

 THE SUPER-OBJECTIVE FOR AN ACTOR IS THE OVERALL GOAL OR OBJECTIVE FOR THE CHARACTER THEY ARE PLAYING. IT IS WITH THEM ALL THE TIME AND NEVER LEAVES THEM.

In other words, the super-objective is what the character *needs* or *wants* in *every* scene it appears. This *need* never changes. It is a *desire* that the character carries with them *all the time*. It is the *inner-pull* on the character that gets them out of bed in the morning. It is the ultimate motivator in the character's life. This is true for all of us in life as well as in acting.

EXERCISE

Answer the following questions:

Q What is your own super-objective in life? In other words, what gets you up in the morning? Or what is your overall goal or goals for your life?

EXERCISE EXERCISE EXERCISE EXERCISE EXERCISE EXERCISE EXERCISE

CHAPTER

FAIL BETTER!

6

> "*Ever tried. Ever failed. No matter.*
> *Try again. Fail again. Fail better.*"
>
> - SAMUEL BECKETT

SUCCESS THROUGH FAILURE

Do you believe you can find success through failure? This supposition seems like an oxymoron, doesn't it? Well, it's not. How many times do you think Thomas Edison "failed" at inventing the light bulb before it finally lit up? How many "failed" flights did the Wright brothers make before they took flight? How many formulas for the theory of relativity do you think Einstein worked on before he came up with $E = mc^2$? In all these cases, I can tell you the answer… *a lot*!

In the hard sciences, the empirical method of trial and error is the expected path toward greater knowledge and is readily accepted as such. Scientists innately understand that it is only through failure that we learn what doesn't work. Once we know what doesn't work then we know what we need to change and improve. Upon first look, the arts can appear a little more ambiguous and conflicted on the matter. Yet, the more time you spend in the arts the more you realize that there is little difference. Keep this in mind during this class. If you can remain open, if you can allow for the possibility of failure, of looking "stupid," of feeling "foolish," of "making an ass out of yourself" then as you begin to process all these keys to acting, you will learn a great deal not only about this art form, but about life, and most importantly, about yourself. You will finish this class with a greater awareness and understanding not only of acting but also of your own existence. That's the point of the arts; they help us live richer, more alert lives.

The most sublimely prescient of all the existential dramatists, Samuel Beckett, said it best, "Fail better." Risking failure is the only way you will learn how to act or grow…so…go ahead…

 "FAIL BETTER!"

PERFECTION

Perfection doesn't exist. It doesn't exist in life. Yet, look around you in your life and you will see many societal pressures to be "perfect": to get the perfect grade, to drive the perfect car, to have the perfect boyfriend or girlfriend, to look "perfect," to live the "perfect" life in the "perfect" neighborhood, etc. But what is perfection anyway? No matter what you come up with, any answer to this question will be incredibly relative and personal. So, why bother? It doesn't exist; so, don't waste your time. It certainly doesn't exist in the arts. What is art but a reflection of life through an idiosyncratic prism? So, it can be said that perfection doesn't exist in art either. What does exist, however, is exactitude and precision in the chosen method of expression. We will talk about this in greater detail later in the book.

The French neo-classicist painter Eugene Delacroix weighed in on this topic over 300 years ago. He said

"ARTISTS WHO SEEK PERFECTION IN EVERYTHING ARE THOSE WHO CANNOT ATTAIN IT IN ANYTHING."

What does this mean for you in this class? It means that there is no such thing as a perfect actor or a perfect performance. By its very nature, acting involves one of the frailties of being human: fallibility. Paradoxically, it is the actor who fully understands this and embraces their vulnerability and fallibility who is usually the most successful. The reason for this is that we go to the theatre to have a human experience, to feel something. As audience members, we crave to empathize with other characters, with their plight, their challenges, their triumphs, their loves, their failures. Actors are professional human beings, which means they need to have all aspects of the human condition at their beck and call.

This does not mean, however, that there are no guidelines, definitions, specific techniques, or "keys" to acting. There are many of them. We will talk about a variety of them throughout this book. But they are there only to help the actor as an artist seek greater specificity in their work, and by that we mean greater strength and uniqueness of expression. There are no flat-out "right" or "wrong" ways to act, but there are certain pitfalls to avoid and certain proven techniques to help the actor unleash their full potential as an actor. The way you as a beginning actor should best go about learning these points of craft is by keeping an open mind, trying everything that is asked of you, refraining from quick judgment, and avoiding trying to do things the "right" way, or to seek perfection.

A CHALLENGE

LEAVE YOUR COMFORT ZONES AT HOME. THROW AWAY THE PROVERBIAL PARACHUTE. JUMP OUT OF THE METAPHORICAL PLANE.

ENGAGE YOUR IMAGINATION.

TRY SOMETHING NEW, SCARY, FUN, EXHILARATING, AND NERVE-WRACKING.

TAKE YOUR FLIP-FLOPS OFF AND KILL "WHATEVER...."

SET CLEAR OBJECTIVES FOR THIS CLASS. TAKE ACTION.

ENGAGE YOURSELF, YOUR TEACHERS AND YOUR CLASSMATES.

RAISE YOUR AWARENESS BY LIFTING YOUR GAZE OUT OF THE FAMILIAR. CONNECT
WITH THE OTHERS AROUND YOU.

RISK FAILURE. RISK LOOKING SILLY. RISK BEING WRONG. FAIL BETTER...

NO MATTER HOW SCARY IT IS!

If you're not prepared to do all of the above, then acting is probably not for you. But if you are, then you are about to embark on one of the most exiting, rewarding, and fulfilling classes of your life.

EXERCISE

Answer the following questions:

Q Why are you afraid of failure?

Q What happens when you fail?

Q What happens when you think you are going to fail and you actually succeed?

Exercise TO DO: This week choose an activity at which you are certain you will fail! Attempt to do what you choose. Use the space below to write your reactions to what you learned through this process.

CHAPTER

RESPECT

7

> *"That title of respect which the proud*
> *soul ne'er pays but to the proud."*
>
> - WILLIAM SHAKESPEARE, *HENRY V*

RESPECT

To stand in front of a group of strangers and say your name aloud with truth and honesty may be the most daunting assignment you have ever had. This alone may be a victory for you in this class. To shed the social mask of adolescence—or whatever age—and act on imaginative and creative impulses, even if only for a moment, may be a victory. I consider it so, and so will your teacher. It will take many different types of respect on your part for you to succeed: respect for art; respect for acting; respect for your professor; respect for your classmates; and ultimately, respect for yourself.

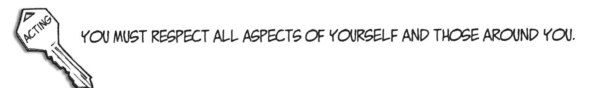

YOU MUST RESPECT ALL ASPECTS OF YOURSELF AND THOSE AROUND YOU.

But you will also need to be respectful of something I'm sure no one has ever asked to respect: your *intuition*. In other words, acting demands that you follow your human impulses. This means getting in touch with the more innate side of yourself. This means putting away the critical, analytical left side of your brain that likes to organize life and compartmentalize it. You will need to respect the half of your brain that is intuitive and illogical. You will need to learn to get in touch with the right side of your brain. And I guarantee you that as soon as you start to do this, the left side of your brain, the analytical side, will make a lot of noise in protest.

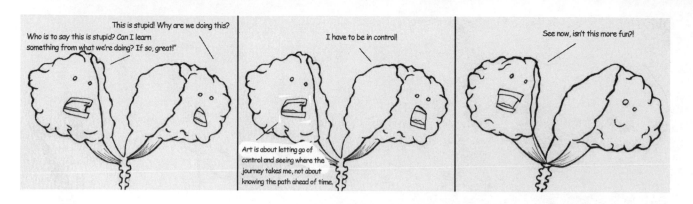

- The left side of the brain will say: "This is stupid! Why are we doing this?"
- The left side of the brain will say: "This doesn't make sense!"
- The left side of the brain will say: "I'll look silly and foolish if I do what the teacher is asking of me!"
- The left side of the brain will say: "I have to be right!"
- The left side of the brain will say: "I have to know the answer!"
- The left side of the brain will say: "I have to be in control!"

And you will have to nurture the right side of your brain, the intuitive side, the side that is neglected by the American education system and our society at large; and you will have to listen to what the right side answers to the left.

- The right side of your brain will answer: "Who is to say this is stupid? Can I learn something from what we're doing? If so, great!"
- The right side of your brain will answer: "Art is not about making sense; it is about creating from your soul, not your intellect."
- The right side of your brain will answer: "I only look foolish if I let other people define who I am."
- The right side of your brain will answer: "Right and wrong has no place in art."
- The right side of your brain will answer: "Art is about living in the question, not having the answer."
- The right side of your brain will answer: "Art is about letting go of control and seeing where the journey takes me, not about knowing the path ahead of time."
- The right side of your brain will ask the left side: "See now, isn't this more fun?!"

YOU MUST DEVELOP AND NURTURE RESPECT FOR THE RIGHT SIDE OF YOUR BRAIN AND YOUR INTUITIVE INSTINCTS AND IMPULSES.

The famous architect-turned-theatre director Robert Wilson put it this way,

"THE REASON WE WORK IN THEATRE IS TO SAY 'WHAT IS IT?' NOT TO SAY, WHAT IT IS."

RESPECT FOR SELF

But none of this can happen unless you start by having respect for yourself:

- You must respect yourself enough to allow for the fact that you might not know the answer to the question at hand. That's why you are in the class: to grow.
- You must respect yourself enough to know that fear of failure is normal. Yet, it is only by moving through fear that you will seize your full potentiality as a human being.
- You must respect yourself enough to know that self-doubt is normal. Everyone experiences it. It comes from the need to get things right all the time. Successful people are those who learn how to productively deal with self-doubt.
- You must respect yourself enough to accomplish all the things that are asked of you in this class. What you do—the effort you put into your work—is after all a direct reflection on who you are as a person.
- You must respect your education enough to validate the choice to take this class by showing up on time and ready to work!

RESPECT FOR YOUR CLASSMATES

It should go without saying you need to respect your classmates. But what does that mean exactly?

- Respect for your classmates means not disturbing the class by arriving late. Show up and be ready to work at the scheduled time.
- Respect for your classmates means treating them professionally and with kindness.
- Respect for your classmates means not talking when they are talking.
- Respect for your classmates means not laughing at them or making fun of them if they make a bold or revealing choice in an exercise.
- Respect for your classmates means doing your share of the work if you are given a group assignment.

RESPECT FOR YOUR PROFESSOR

It should REALLY go without saying that you must respect your professor! But let's cover a couple gentle reminders of what this means in case your memory needs refreshing:

- Respect for your professor means being ready to work at the appointed class time with your mobile phones turned off (not on vibrate) and put away.
- Respect for your professor means giving them your undivided attention.
- Respect for your professor means not talking with your friend during class time.
- Respect for your professor means getting your work done on time.
- Respect for your professor means actively participating in the class with a positive attitude.
- Respect for your professor means being proactive to help to create a constructive and supportive environment for everyone.

RESPECT FOR ACTING

And finally, you must have respect for the art form of acting. What does this mean?

- Respect for acting means recognizing that there is more to it than meets the eye.

- Respect for acting means understanding that this is an art form and not a reality television show.

- Respect for acting means committing fully to the exercises and assignments in class if you are going to learn anything about this art form.

- Respect for acting means listening and accepting ideas and theories that may seem foreign to you at first.

- Respect for acting means behaving in a mature and professional manner in class.

- Respect for acting means behaving in a mature and professional manner in the theatre while viewing the shows.

EXERCISE

Answer the following questions:

Q What is respect? How do you define it?

Q What are the things, people or ideas that you respect in your life?

Q List three ways in which you could respect yourself more.

Q List the ways in which respect influences our work in this class.

EXERCISE EXERCISE EXERCISE EXERCISE EXERCISE EXERCISE EXERCISE

CHAPTER 8

TRUST

> *"It is impossible to go through life without trust: that is to be imprisoned in the worst cell of all, oneself."*
>
> - GRAHAM GREEN

TRUST

The many facets of trust are all equally essential ingredients to successful acting, or for that matter any challenging endeavor in life. Fundamentally, all the components of trust boil down to believing in either yourself or other people. In the case of actors, they must believe not only in their talent, technique, and ability to perform the part, but they must also trust the vision of the director who is helming their project, as well as all the other actors and designers with whom they are working to fulfill this vision. An actor who works without trust will end up closing themselves off in an isolated performance bubble shaped by cliché, habit, and indicating. In a nutshell, trust is confidence. You either have it in yourself or other people, or you don't. But it certainly can be worked on and developed like the other tools of acting.

TRUST YOUR SELF

It should go without saying that an actor needs to have trust in him- or herself in order to create character successfully. Yet, often this is one of the hardest things for many actors to master or come to terms with. Trust in self, a sure path to confidence, can be a slippery eel. Sometimes you have it, sometimes you don't. On stage or in front of a camera, confidence comes from knowing what to do and being able to do it. This requires enormous amounts of training, technique, experience, and preparation. The blend of all these things leads to confidence in performance. But trust is the cement that holds them all together. It doesn't matter how much training, experience, or technique an actor has, if they don't trust their abilities when they walk out on stage they will be hard pressed to find ease, truthfulness, and confidence in their work. Acting without trust in self is a painfully difficult exercise. The actor who doesn't trust him- or herself will be more worried about whether or not they are doing a good job or whether they are making the right or wrong choices. The actor who works with trust surrenders to the moment and has an inner confidence, even if they are nervous, that the work, preparation, training, and experience they have stored up to this point will serve them when they need it. It is a symbiotic relationship, and all the components are interdependent. It is difficult to have trust in self or in one's own ability without the composite of training, technique, and experience. Consequently, they all feed off of one another and support each other. Growth in one area can lead to exponential leaps in another and vice versa. Clearly, the more an actor trusts that he or she knows precisely what to do in any given performance situation, the more likely they are to work with confidence.

Also, if you don't trust yourself that means you somehow doubt yourself. Doubt does no one any good, especially you. Imagine the following: If you had a choice, would you prefer to work with another actor who trusted their ability or doubted it? Would you prefer to work with an actor who trusted their colleagues or doubted them? Would you prefer to work with a director who trusted his or her own vision or one who doubted it? I think the answer is obvious. We would all prefer to work with other individuals who trust their own ability as well as those with whom they are working. The same goes for you. Your colleagues would much prefer that you trust your abilities rather than doubt them, even if you don't have all that much experience or training. This may be obvious, yes, yet it is often the most obvious things that demand the most attention. A helpful acting teacher builds the actor's confidence not only by teaching technique but also by engendering trust in the work and pushing the perceived limits of the student's abilities.

TRUST YOUR CLASSMATES

Just as in a professional show it is essential in an acting class that the students trust one another. Acting is an incredibly personal art form, one that demands revelation of self and enormous amounts of risk in the doing. If the students of an acting class don't trust each other, for whatever reason, then they will remain closed off to one another. Ensemble building, which is an important part of what any director does with a performance project, is necessary in the classroom as well. Just imagine if you felt that your classmates were judging you and ridiculing you when you worked instead of supporting you. You probably wouldn't feel much like taking risks in front of them. And, as we've already discussed, no risk, no growth. So much of what goes on in any classroom, but especially an acting studio, revolves around trust. It is of paramount importance that each one of you trusts the other. The next time someone in the class is working, even someone you don't know at all, give them your full attention and support. Help them to do a better job by caring about their work rather than just taking care of your own work. If each member of your class follows your lead, then that class will come to a place of trust and security. I guarantee you that all the work in the class will be that much more rewarding.

TRUST YOUR PROFESSOR

Again, it seems like an obvious statement, something that shouldn't need to be said, but you will need to place an enormous amount of trust in your professor. Yes, trust must be earned, but it can also be given. As the teachers are the ones guiding your work, you must surrender to this guidance even if the exercises make you feel uncomfortable or embarrassed. Much of actor training involves coaxing actors out of their protective shells and pushing them beyond their safety zones. The good acting teacher will create an atmosphere of trust and permissiveness in the classroom, thereby encouraging the emergence over time of collective and individual trust. This openness can lead the students to perform beyond what they believe their means are. But the professor must earn the trust of the student as well. They must set the bar high for the student by leading by example. If they do this in all earnestness and integrity, however, then it is up to the student to return that trust so their work can bear the fruit of growth. It is ultimately up to the student to trust in themselves, the work, their classmates and the professor enough to take the leap of faith. Trust will billow the proverbial parachute and lead you to a safe landing in exciting new territory way outside of your comfort zones. Trust me!

"USE THE FORCE, LUKE. LET GO, LUKE. LUKE, TRUST ME." — STAR WARS, GEORGE LUCAS

CHAPTER 9

RISK

"A lot of people refuse to do things because they don't want to go naked, don't want to go without guarantee. But that's what's got to happen. You go naked until you die."

- NIKKI GIOVANNI

RISK

You've undoubtedly heard the truism, "Nothing risked, nothing gained." Indeed, there is no growth without risk, whether we are talking about the stock market, sports, the arts, or dating. Risk and growth are directly correlated. This correlation is definitely applicable to acting. The question is always: How much can you risk? Another way of asking the same question is: How much can you afford to lose? That then begs the question: What is risk or loss in acting? The answer to this is as varied as the number of actors risking something. But before we look at the risks involved, remember the following key:

 RISK NOTHING, GAIN NOTHING!

Acting by definition involves personal risk. It is not for the faint of heart. If you are going to grow in this class, and thereby begin to learn what it is exactly that actors do, then you will have to risk something. Actors take risks every time they go on an audition, rehearse, or act in a piece. Every time they work they put their acting choices out there for other people to judge. Every singe time! For example, you might be afraid of looking foolish in front of your classmates. Can you imagine if an actor on a popular primetime television show worried about the same thing? They would be paralyzed creatively by the fear of looking stupid. And they aren't just in front of a room full of people; they are literally acting out their choices in front of tens of millions of people across the country, plus re-runs and DVD rentals! That's a lot of people to have to not worry about!

The actor must act boldly. They must make strong choices. They must be brave and confident in the execution of their work. Acting demands emotional, vocal, psychological, and physical risks of vulnerability. An actor has to live in his or her imagination. Actors have to commit themselves without restraint to all aspects of the parts they play. The creative choices they make in service of the character must be important and meaningful. Occasionally, as we have mentioned, these choices can seem foolish to the average lay person, one who don't understand the actor's process. Actors accept that one of the inherent risks of being an actor is being judged by onlookers, perhaps even of looking foolish. They quickly learn to develop a thick skin and figure out which comments are constructive and which are not. Those who can't ever get over this hurdle never become actors. Ultimately, they place too much store in other people's opinions to be a true artist. Actors can't afford to do this. Too much is at stake.

 BY FEARING WHAT OTHERS MIGHT SAY ABOUT YOU, YOU EMPOWER THEM AND LIMIT YOURSELF.

A quote from one of the legendary American acting teachers of the twentieth century, Mr. Sanford Meisner, addresses this issue:

 "ACTING REQUIRES THE PURE, UNSELFCONSCIOUS REVELATION OF THE GIFTED ACTOR'S MOST INNER AND MOST PRIVATE BEING TO THE PEOPLE IN HIS AUDIENCE."

The risk I am asking you to take here is to let go of the desire to concern yourself with how you are doing what you are asked to do, and as the old Nike advertising campaign went:

 JUST DO IT!

THE VOCATION OF ACTING

It is often said in acting schools, "If you think you can possibly do something else with your life and be happy doing it, then you probably shouldn't be an actor." I agree. Acting is not for everyone. By that I mean the life of an actor is not for everyone. Spend enough time with professional actors and I guarantee that you will hear someone say:

 "ACTING IS A VOCATION, NOT AN OCCUPATION."

What they mean by this is that it is not just a job. For most actors I know it is a calling, a way of life. It is something they "must do." Acting is something very real that actors are drawn to, most of the time against all common sense and financial security. A life as an actor involves great uncertainty and risk. The only guarantee in acting is that there is none. However, that said, to return to the original premise of this chapter, because the *risk* is so great, so is the *reward*. Nothing worth doing in life is ever easy. A fulfilling life as an actor will challenge any monetary rewards offered by most other professions. But it will not come without sacrifice and hardship. There comes with being an actor much uncertainty. There comes with being an actor long stretches of unemployment. There comes with being an actor countless rejections at auditions. But if you have the inner artistic fire, the mental tenacity and psychological fortitude to handle these tempestuous waters, then there also comes something else with being an actor that is priceless. It is what the French call a *raison d'etre*, or "reason to be."

If there is one gift I would give all my students, it would be this: for them to find their "life's work," their own *raison d'etre*. For once you have that, no one can take it away.

In the words of George Bernard Shaw:

 "SELF-BETRAYAL, MAGNIFIED TO SUIT THE OPTICS OF THE THEATRE, IS THE WHOLE ART OF ACTING."

EXERCISE

Answer the following questions:

Q What would be the biggest risk you could take in this class? Why?

Q What is the biggest risk you could take right now in your life?

EXERCISE EXERCISE EXERCISE EXERCISE EXERCISE EXERCISE EXERCISE

CHAPTER

INDIVIDUALITY 10

> *"Since you are like no other being ever created since the beginning of time— you are incomparable."*
>
> - Brenda Ueland

INDIVIDUALITY

Much of our energy in life is spent conforming to societal norms. We wear the same clothes. We watch the same TV shows. We eat the same food. We drive the same cars. We buy the same material items. We live in identical "cookie cutter" communities. Conformity is a valued commodity in any society, for it encourages unity and perhaps, idealistically, utopian harmony. Conformity is presently spreading like wildfire across the globe. In doing it has certainly made lives more convenient, but important cultural differences and identities are rapidly evaporating before our very eyes. Since the advent of ubiquitous air travel, and more recently the Internet, the world has perceptively and figuratively shrunk. European countries have lost their individual currencies in favor of the Euro; McDonalds has infested every corner of the globe from Prague to Pnom Pen; kids in Afghanistan listen to American Rap music, wear bling-bling jewelry; and there are a half-dozen companies that make all the cars in the world. Is the planet really a better place for all this homogenization? Is a Big Mac better than a crepe Parisian for lunch? Is a New York Yankee hat better than a burka? Is a Hollywood summer blockbuster movie better than an independent Iranian film? There are as many answers to these questions as there are subjective opinions. However, they hopefully make you think about the world around you and what it is becoming.

On a meta-level, the world is certainly more convenient. But is it better for it? Right or wrong, sane arguments can be made for both sides. But what is undisputedly happening is that many defining societal components, those that provide any country with its unique identity, are slowly melting away in the name of convenience and modernity. In a nutshell, literally the world we live in is becoming less diverse. For the most part, societies are moving toward a greater global conformity. And those countries that don't agree with the macro-movement of what has become to be known as the global market are moving in a different direction because they don't want to conform with the values of the rest of the world.

Look around the room at your classmates, your family, and your communities. Do you recognize this to be true from your own experience? Do you see conformity in your lives? Or perhaps you live in and come from a very diverse family or community. How would you feel if the diversity in your community was surgically removed? Well, it's happening. Just watch over the next twenty years how the world changes even faster.

Have you ever heard of the "Golden Arches Theory of Conflict Prevention?" *The New York Times* op-ed author, Pulitzer Prize winner, Thomas L. Friedman in his book *The Lexus and The Olive Tree* coined this theory. He accurately and astutely observed that no two countries with a McDonald's franchise had ever gone to war with one another. This is a gastronomic alternate version of the democratic peace theory, albeit, unfortunately, a fast food, super-size-me one. Until the brief NATO bombing of Serbia in 1999, Friedman's theory held true. Even so, the conflict was swift, and ultimately Serbia wanted to remain a part of the global economy; so, it was all over fairly quickly.

Why do you think this is so? Could it be that on some primordial level we crave conformity and homogeneity? Is it that we deeply feel the need to be "like" others? The empirical answers to these questions can be found around campus in the fields of sociology, anthropology, psychology, and economics. Yet the aspect of this question that the arts deal with is the authentic "voice" of the individual in society—the *non*-conformist.

THE NON-CONFORMIST

Did you know that the following people were considered non-conformist during the times in which they walked the earth?

- Socrates
- Plato
- Aristotle
- Jesus
- Buddha
- Leonardo da Vinci
- Galileo

- Thomas Edison
- Claude Monet
- Charlie Parker
- The Beatles
- Elvis
- Andy Warhol
- Marlon Brando

…and many others. What would the world be without these creative forces? What would the world look like? What would we think like? Would we still believe that the world is flat?

In extreme societies, as well as many orthodox religions, individuality is discouraged. Why do you think this is? Could it be perhaps that if you had a country of individual thinkers and doers it would be hard to control what they think and do? Probably so! And yet, what do you get if everyone thinks, acts, dresses, behaves, believes, and does things the same way? I wager…the most boring and unimaginative world ever!

It is the job of the arts—and therefore artists—to challenge societal norms, or at least, as the title character in Williams Shakespeare's tragedy *Hamlet* says to,

"HOLD A MIRROR UP TO NATURE."

Examine the famous quote by the late nineteenth-century German existentialist philosopher Friedrich Nietzsche:

"ART RAISES ITS HEAD WHERE CREEDS RELAX."

EXERCISE

Answer the following question:

What do you think Nietzsche meant by this? Take a moment and write down your thoughts on his statement about art.

All successful dictators, fascists, and ideologues have understood that to maintain power they must destroy or control the arts. Why were such powerful twentieth-century dictators such as Adolf Hitler, Joseph Stalin, and Benito Mussolini afraid of the arts? Why did they feel the need to eradicate the artists and then create their own "state-sponsored" art? What were these hugely powerful men with potent military forces at their beck and call so afraid of in the artist? What was the United States congress of the mid-1990s afraid of when they cut the National Endowment for the Arts budget to shreds?

I will tell you. They feared:

 INDIVIDUALITY

THINK OUT OF THE BOX

Why do they all fear individuality in society? Because individualism is a power more mighty than any army. All successful demagogues (and/or advertising executives) have understood that if you can break a person's individuality you can control their feelings, thoughts, and actions (or purchases).

So, what does any of this have to do with acting, you might ask yourself?

Individuality has everything to do with acting because

WHO YOU ARE,

WHAT YOU BELIEVE IN,

WHAT YOU STAND FOR,

WHAT YOU HAVE TO SAY,

WHAT YOU IMAGINE,

WHAT YOU DESIRE TO CREATE IS THE REALM OF THE ARTS!

INDIVIDUALITY IN ACTING

Individuality is everything in acting. Who you are is essentially what is going to get you hired as an actor, especially in Los Angeles where there is a higher premium on personality actors than character actors. (We'll get into the difference between the two more specifically later on.) Even so, who you are is the end-all be-all in acting. One of the many paradoxes of the art of acting involves the intricate and delicate dance between your "self" and the "character" you are playing. It is one of the eternal questions in acting—or in any art: Where does "self" end and "character" begin? (We will take up this paradox in greater detail later as well. However, it's worth mentioning here.)

In a sense, all "technique" does is help an artist express themselves more fully, no matter their preferred medium of expression. Acting methods only serve to release a greater range of expression and dimension in the actor's natural ability. Technique gives foundation, consistency, breadth, and range to innate individual talent. If that individual talent isn't there to begin with, technique won't have much with which to work.

 AN ACTOR'S INDIVIDUAL TALENT IS WHAT THEY BRING TO EVERY ROLE THEY PLAY.

Listen to the wise, encouraging words from the seminal force in modern dance, Martha Graham:

 "THERE IS A VITALITY, A LIFE FORCE, AN ENERGY, A QUICKENING THAT IS TRANSLATED THROUGH YOU INTO ACTION, AND BECAUSE THERE IS ONLY ONE OF YOU IN ALL TIME, THIS EXPRESSION IS UNIQUE. IF YOU BLOCK IT, IT WILL BE LOST AND NEVER EXIST THROUGH ANY OTHER MEDIUM."

- MARTHA GRAHAM

EXERCISE

Answer the following questions:

Q You may not consider yourself to be an artist necessarily, but you are an individual. List the things you bring to the table that define your uniqueness.

Q Use the space below to identify the areas of conformity in your life.

CHAPTER

> "(O I see what I sought to escape,
> confronting, reversing my cries,
> I see my own soul trampling down
> what it ask'd for.)
>
> Keep your splendid silent sun,
> Keep your woods O Nature,
> and the quiet places by the woods,
> Keep your fields of clover and timothy,
> and your corn-fields and orchards,
> Keep the blossoming buckwheat fields
> where the Ninth-month bees hum;
> Give me faces and streets—give me
> these phantoms incessant and
> endless along the trottoirs!"
>
> - WALT WHITMAN

HUMAN CONNECTION

This acting class may be one of the most challenging and rewarding experiences you will have during your college experience. Not only is it consistently one of the most popular courses on university campuses from coast to coast, but it also provides you with an indelible *human experience*, one that you may never replicate in other classrooms, even perhaps throughout the rest of your life. The importance of this class on a *human level* is not to be overlooked. *Human connection* is the essential magic of acting. It is also one of the greatest tools you can carry forward into your life no matter what field you end up in. I truly believe if more people took acting classes there would be less conflict and more understanding in the world. It is my hope that you will better understand what I mean by this by the end of this course and ultimately agree.

PSYCHOLOGICAL THEATRE IS AN ATTEMPT TO UNDERSTAND ANOTHER PERSON AS
YOURSELF.

- SLAVA DOLGACHEV

Over the trajectory of this class you will experience many emotions: highs and lows; joys and frustrations; triumphs and failures; fears and discoveries. You will learn an enormous amount, not only about acting and its core techniques, but also about *yourself as a human being*. Unbeknownst to you, you will touch many lives. You will change how you see yourself, others around, you and the world at large.

 YOUR OWN LIFE WILL BE TOUCHED AND CHANGED PROFOUNDLY.

I guarantee it. For this is what artists do, touch other people—be they actors, musicians, painters, writers, sculptors, or poets.

HUMAN ENGAGEMENT

Acting is about the human condition. It is about humanity. It is about human beings. To be an actor you must be more aware of those around you than the average person. An actor must be more sensitive to behavior and human psychology. To be successful as an actor you have to have a deep craving for human engagement.

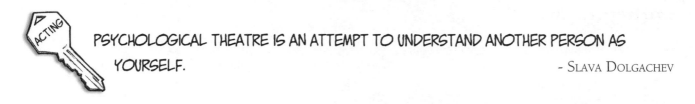 THE DEGREE TO WHICH YOU TOUCH OTHERS IS DIRECTLY CORRELATED TO THE DEGREE
TO WHICH YOU MAKE YOURSELF AVAILABLE TO THE HUMAN EXPERIENCE.

Most of you may never go on to further studies in acting or theatre arts. Many of you may never have set foot in a theatre before this class. Perhaps you are drawn to acting by dreams of stardom in film and television. There is nothing wrong with that. No matter what level of experience you have with acting at the beginning of this class—even if that means only what you have seen on television—you can still learn about what it is real actors do and what it means to belong to the art of acting. But to do so you must open yourself up and make yourself available to your professor and your peers. This is what actors do.

Whether your realize it or not, your ability to pull your *attention* away from your mobile phones or electronic games when coming into class, or when taking your seat in the theatre and redirecting it onto other *human beings* may be a major victory. In doing so, you will lift your gaze out from the disconnected world of cold, metallic technology and look into the warm eyes of other *people*. You will become a part of the *collective human gathering* known as the theatre.

 ACTING IS ABOUT ENGAGING OTHER PEOPLE.

SHOWING UP

Acting demands that you be actively engaged in the doing. To "do" you need to be "present." To quote Aristotle:

 "TO BE IS TO DO."

To engage other people, you have to show up—you have to actually be in the room and clear of mind. There is no "show" if you don't "show up." Acting is doing. And if you aren't in class, you can't do. It's that simple. No do, no grow. This is not a subject where you can miss half the classes and then get the notes from someone else in the hopes of learning something. Anything substantive in life demands full engagement as a human being, physical and mental. That means showing up on both levels. If the show is to go on, it needs you!

 ACTING IS ABOUT SHOWING UP.

EXERCISE

Answer the following questions:

Exercise TO DO: Over the next week as you walk around campus notice when people do or don't make eye contact. Although, it may seem a little uncomfortable, force yourself to make eye contact with a variety of different people. Make yourself open and available to the people in your community and see what happens. What do you observe from these simple exchanges?

CHAPTER

> *"Man is least himself when he talks in his own person. Give him a mask, and he will tell you the truth."*
>
> - OSCAR WILDE

SOCIAL MASKS

We act all day, every day, every single one of us. Throughout our lives we play many parts: son, daughter, friend, lover, enemy, student, teammate, parent, teacher, employee, boss, etc. We wear different social masks for each of these roles because "*who we are*" is a complex matrix of differing and complex variables. Rarely do we act the same way in any of these parts. We constantly and subtlety shift gears based on the *circumstances* we find ourselves in and relationships to those people around us while we are in those circumstances. We are good at it because it comes naturally to us and we have been doing it since we were children. Even as infants we innately knew how to cry a certain way to get what we wanted. Yet as intuitive as it may seem, recreating behavior consciously, which is what an actor does, is a complex and multi-dimensional art form, one that is quite often misunderstood by the general public.

Over the course of this class you will come to understand how we operate from behind the daily masks we wear. You will learn to turn these masks into powerful tools to play the role you *wish* to play to its fullest potential, even if you never become a professional actor. For *playing* involves *action*. And *act-ion* is the heart of *act-ing*. And the actions we take depend on what we want from the people we are with in the circumstances we find ourselves in. If you can grasp this than you can understand the foundational elements of what an actor does.

Social Mask Woman !!!

EXERCISE

Answer the following questions:

Q Can you identify three different social masks you wear in your own life?

Q Do you think these masks reveal or hide your true feelings?

CHAPTER

ATTENTION AND CONCENTRATION 13

> *"The soul is not a soul,*
> *Has no secret, is small, and it fits*
> *Its hollow perfectly: its room, our moment*
> *of attention."*
>
> - JOHN ASHBERY

ATTENTION

If you want to grow you have to apply your attention to that aspect of your life in which you want to see change. A plant needs water and sunlight to survive. If you don't *pay attention* to it by placing it in the right amount of sunlight and don't water it appropriately it won't grow. In fact it will eventually wither and die. Why? It will die because you neglected it. And what is neglect, but the absence of *attention*?

Conversely, let's say you go to the gym three days a week for a year, which is generally recommended. But each time you go, you put all your attention on only one part of your body. Let's say all you ever do is work on your quads. You will definitely see growth in your thighs by the end of that year. But to what end? Your legs will look out of proportion to the rest of your body. In this case you would have mistakenly put your attention on one aspect of your physique to the detriment of the rest of your body. And you would look like this...

We have the expression to "pay attention" in our English lexicon. We use the word "pay" because attention has intrinsic *value*. Your attention is *worth* something, not only to your professors and fellow classmates but also to you. It has *currency*. Don't throw your attention away. Even if you were ridiculously rich you wouldn't toss cold cash away, would you? No, of course not, unless you were foolish. So don't waste your attention either. It's valuable. Treat it so.

When you come to this class, if you want to grow, you will have to *shape* your attention to meet the demands of the day. By this I mean that you will have to *give* your attention to your teacher and your fellow classmates, or *put* it on some aspect of your imagination, voice, or body. Seems simple. But then again the most important values in life are quite simple, and bear repeating. So…let me repeat.

 GROWTH HAPPENS WHERE YOU PUT YOUR ATTENTION.

In this class, as in your entire life, I encourage you to actively apply your attention to the tasks at hand, and to do so in amounts distributed equally and appropriately.

TARGETS OF ATTENTION

In his seminal book on acting, *The Actor and the Target*, British director Declan Donnellan states that success as an actor depends wholly on where the actor's attention is placed. This is true. We will talk about this at greater length later in this book, but for now I want to introduce to you the following concept.

 YOUR ATTENTION NEEDS A TARGET.

When we "pay attention" what is it we actually do? We give ourselves a singular point of focus. We concentrate our attention onto the task or subject at hand. For example, ask yourself honestly, are you really paying attention to what you are reading right now? Chances are you aren't, or your attention is split with something else. Do you have other things on your mind? Are you thinking about things in the past? What you are going to do later today? Are you daydreaming? Does the environment in which you are reading distract you? Although multi-tasking is the *lingua franca* of our era, it still remains true that quality work gets done when you put all your attention on one thing at a time.

 "BETTER A LITTLE WHICH IS WELL DONE, THAN A GREAT DEAL IMPERFECTLY." - PLATO

The world we inhabit is becoming increasingly complex and makes more and more demands on our attention with each passing year. Simply put, our world is a more distracted place to live than it was even 20 years ago. Consequently, we are becoming more distracted as a people. Advances in technology, although providing our lives with greater convenience, often challenge our ability to concentrate. We live in the fast-paced world of Attention Deficit Disorder, video games, flashing spots, pop-up ads, sound bites, running news banners on television screens, text messages, and—as if a text message wasn't fast enough—the *instant* message. All these things, plus many more, compete for our attention every second we're awake. It is no wonder so many people today have a hard time focusing. However, they can focus if they literally set their minds to it. They just have to been shown how. I know of no métier worth studying that doesn't require a foundation of concentration. Most people flit their concentration away as if it were an endless commodity, readily replenishable. It's not. Your attention and concentration are a precious commodity and should be treated as such.

For example, how much time during the day do you *spend*—there's that monetary analogy again—with your attention buried in your mobile phone, video-game, or Myspace account? To what benefit? Again, no value judgment here, just ask yourself to objectively note the truth. What do you actually gain from putting your attention on these areas of your life? Are you *aware* of how much time you are *spending* on these things? Chances are you spend and expend an enormous amount of attention in these areas. Most of these targets of our attention offer limited growth opportunities. The first step in affecting greater growth is to identify the areas of your life that act as black holes for your attention and then eliminate them, or at least reduce the amount of your attention that you allot to those areas of your life.

CONCENTRATION

Once you have found a target for your attention, the next step is to keep it there. Concentration is the ability to maintain mental focus on the target of your attention. It is also one of the foundations of actor training. Essentially, all other work flows from this indispensable skill. At the end of the day, if an actor can't concentrate on their technique, scene partner, performance, or career, they won't have much success. I would dare to say that this holds true for just about any challenging field of study. As we have already established, your ability to grow depends on the target of your attention. The amount of growth you experience is determined by your ability to concentrate on that target.

 CONCENTRATION IS THE FOUNDATION OF ACTOR TRAINING!

One of the simplest things you can do to increase your ability to concentrate is SLOW DOWN! Inevitably, you have heard the saying,

 SLOW DOWN AND SMELL THE ROSES.

As we all know, roses are one of the most pleasantly pungent odors in the floral kingdom. Yet, you can't smell them if you're running by. And you're libel to get a nice scratch across your face if you approach the bush too quickly. The point is that the quality of the rose's scent can only be appreciated by slowing down. Literally, it is designed that way. In our fast food culture, slowing down is certainly underappreciated. The executives at McDonalds might begin to worry if we all slowed down enough to truly smell the roses of their pre-processed plant! They are counting on us to go quickly so we don't really *pay attention* to what it is we're eating!

In summary, in order to pay attention you need to actively place your attention on a focused target, and you must do so with concentration. The more you slow down, the easier all this it will be. Additionally, once you slow down, the more curious you are about your target, and the easier it will be to concentrate. Remember our chapter on curiosity?

 "CONCENTRATION IS THE SECRET OF STRENGTH IN POLITICS, IN WAR, IN TRADE, IN SHORT IN ALL MANAGEMENT OF HUMAN AFFAIRS."

- RALPH WALDO EMERSON

SELF-CONSCIOUSNESS

Self-consciousness is death to the actor. The more self-conscious an actor is, the worse their performance will be. Guaranteed. Why do you suppose this is? One of the reasons is simply, by definition, if you are "self" conscious your attention is on yourself and not on achieving your objective. You can't pursue your objective if you are thinking about yourself, or if you are worried how you look. If you are concerned with how you are doing—whatever it is you are doing—when you act then that is literally what you are doing: *You are concerning yourself with your "self."* And this is not the type of "doing" that moves the character closer to obtaining their objective. Objectives are obtained by going after them relentlessly and single-mindedly, by what actors call by "*playing action.*" In most circumstances in life, and certainly in virtually all of dramatic literature, this implies taking action *vis á vis* the person with whom you are in the "scene." That means you *target* them with your *concentrated attention* and *change them* to get what it is you want, need, or desire. You change THEM. You change THEM. You change THEM.

 ACTING IS CHANGING THE OTHER PERSON IN FRONT OF YOU!

If your *attention* is on *yourself*—or *what* you are doing, or how you are doing what you are doing—then you can't take action to win your objective. What you are actually doing when you are self-conscious is placing your attention on yourself; you are concerned with how you are being perceived by the audience, your peers, your director, or your professor. This will drive any actor right out of creative state of mind and usher them right into the "Bad acting camp for boys and girls!"

Can you *risk* putting all your *attention* on your scene partner and not yourself? In the current world of "My"space, "i"pod, "me" generation, and "on demand," everything might be harder than it seems at first blush. Acting will test your ability to forget about yourself when working in front of a room full of people. But I can tell you the one sure-fire way to forget about yourself: Put all your attention somewhere else.

THE PINK ELEPHANT CONUNDRUM

You've surely heard the old saying about the pink elephant in the room. It bears repeating here. If you say to someone, "Don't think about that pink elephant in the room drinking tea," chances are that all they will be able to think about is that pink elephant in the room drinking tea. Why? The reason for this is that by mentioning the word "pink elephant" you have *drawn their attention to it*. By telling them NOT to do something, you have inadvertently made them think about it again, albeit for a split second. But if you really don't want someone to think about the pink elephant in the room, the best thing to do is to draw their attention to *something else* without ever mentioning the lovely rosé pachyderm delicately sipping Darjeeling on the settee. You should draw the *target* of their attention *elsewhere*, as it were.

SLUUURP!

If we apply this same principle to acting, then what needs to happen is your attention needs to be placed somewhere else so you won't think about yourself. Let me humbly suggest you put it on your scene partner.

PUT ALL YOUR ATTENTION ON YOUR SCENE PARTNER AND YOU WILL BECOME LESS SELF-CONSCIOUS.

This may seem risky and unfamiliar at first, but that's the whole point. Remember, no risk, no gain.

THE ZONE

You hear athletes talk of playing in the "zone." They say that it was "as if" the game "played itself" and they were just a part of the "flow." The effort required to play they say was full of "ease" and "clarity." Time disappeared. The zone is a place of optimum performance. As there are many similarities between sport and the performing arts, the zone principles hold true for acting as well. The type of physical dexterity, mental creativity, training, technique, conditioning, focus, concentration, imagination, composure under pressure, and precise execution in performance that is needed for sport is the same that is needed for acting.

Did you know that the average human being has between 3,000 and 4,000 thoughts per day? Did you also know that the average champion athlete has only between 1,500 and 2,000 thoughts per day? Why is it, do you think, that champions have fewer thoughts? It is because they are focused on fewer things, like what it takes to improve their game in order to be the best, in order to win. The average person clutters their thinking with unnecessary thoughts. These thoughts act as distractions, keeping the average person from achieving their personal best.

By the way, can you guess how many daily thoughts young children have? If you assumed that they have about the same as champions, then you are right. We now know from studies of childhood brain development that the time of greatest and most productive learning is between birth and five years of age. During this time of cerebral fertility, children are unconcerned with judgment. They are free of value assignment, and whether or not they are doing things "right" or "wrong." Their minds are free of contextual restraint and social coding. But ironically it is during this same period that they are learning the social "rules" that will ultimately impede their imaginations and trample on their innate and wonderful naiveté. Babies simply observe, mirror, and refine; observe, mirror, and refine; observe, mirror, and refine. They keep it simple. They don't get in their own way. Take for example the incredibly complex motor task of bi-pedal movement, otherwise known as walking. Have you ever heard of a parent sitting down and explaining the "instructions" to a baby on how to walk? No, of course not. That would be silly. Why? Because what babies do is watch what others do and repeat. The brain contains what are called "mirror neurons" that facilitate behavioral adaptation. The sole purpose of these neurons is to "mirror" behavior from the observed world. So, in a sense, babies let the mirror neurons do all the work for them. They "stay out of the way" of the natural process of learning. They don't "over think it." They, "just do it!" Would that the average acting student would do the same! It would make the work of acting teachers everywhere a lot easier! The task of the teacher, in addition to teaching technique, is to lead the student back to that beautifully open place of the child's mind. What acting teachers do is attempt to re-wire the student's brain to the way it was when they were children. Acting teachers try to help the student "un-do" all the social conditioning that has taken place between childhood and adulthood.

So, what do babies and champions have in common?

BOTH CHAMPIONS AND BABIES WORK AND LIVE IN THE "ZONE."

This single-mindedness of purpose gives both champions and babies a very compelling and attractive target for their attention. Consequently, neither is distracted by the multitude of "unnecessary" thoughts that bog down and cloud the focus of the average human being. Babies focus on one thing at a time; so do athletes. They both do only that which is needed to accomplish the task at hand and nothing more. Let me repeat, they do *nothing more* than is needed at the time. I mean, *nothing* more. They certainly don't muddy the doing with judgment about whether or not they are right or wrong. They just "do"; they note objectively what they did and then ask, "Did I do what I set out to do?" If the answer is "yes," they check off that proverbial box and move on. If the answer is "no," they *objectively* and *dispassionately* ask themselves "Why not?" Then they attempt to figure out what in the doing—or thinking—inhibited them from successful completion of the task. This is called keeping an "objective perspective" on your work. Actors must also have this single-mindedness of purpose and objective perspective if they are going to be successful.

Zone thinking demands single-mindedness of purpose (super-objective). It demands strong and seductive targets of attention for the task at hand (objectives). It demands focused and concentrated thinking and doing (action). It demands focus on improving ability in an area of craft, "technique-consciousness" (not *self-consciousness*). It demands objective perspective (not self-judgment). Simply put, it demands everything of the performer's life; in a word, it demands *sacrifice*. Sacrifice of what, you may ask? It demands sacrifice of "self"…on the alter of the chosen form of performance.

 THE ZONE IS A MENTAL PLACE OF OPTIMUM PERFORMANCE WHERE CONCENTRATION AND EASE MEET TO MAXIMIZE ABILITY.

If you're not up for this sacrifice, that's fine. But if you are going to study acting, you need to grasp that this, and much more, is what is demanded of actors in their art form. Nothing less.

EXERCISE

Answer the following questions:

Q What are the areas of your life where you seem to put the most attention?

Q Exercise TO DO: Right now take the next three minutes to close your eyes and put all of your attention on your breath. Every time your attention wanders, which it will, bring it back to your breath.

Q How successful were you? Did you find it was easy for you to stay focused on your breathing or did your mind constantly wander? Whatever the answer is, begin to develop an awareness of when your mind wanders from what you are actually trying to do.

Q In order to concentrate we must focus all of our attention on our objective. Right now give yourself exactly two minutes to create a list of your teacher's names from kindergarten through high school.

Q **Exercise TO DO:** Visualization – Spend the next five minutes visualizing your childhood bedroom. Try to visualize as many details as possible, leaving nothing out.

CHAPTER 14

AWARENESS

> *"Nobody sees a flower—really—it is so small it takes time—we haven't time—and to see takes time, like to have a friend takes time."*
>
> - GEORGIA O'KEEFFE

AREAS OF AWARENESS

Actor training is all about awareness. This is universally what any acting school strives to enhance in the actor. Training is usually divided into two areas, each of which has multiple subsets. The two areas of work are on the "self" and on the "role." Usually a serious training regimen begins by increasing awareness of the actor's instrument—the physical, vocal, sensory, emotional, and energy components. These initial areas of development constitute work on the "self."

The training then continues with increasing specificity by working on areas of technique. Acting techniques for the most part tend to match dramatic writing styles; these include, but are not limited to, Shakespeare, psychological realism, theatre of the Absurd, Existentialism, Brecht, Restoration Comedy, Commedia Dell'Arte, etc. Yet technique also includes approaches to work in the mediums of theatre, film, and television. Each of these different mediums demands particular adjustments in distance of communication. Actors must know the techniques dictated by the writing and then adjust their instrument according to those needs and the particular medium in which they are working. This second portion of the training, the technique, represents work on the "role."

If the actor is not acutely cognoscente of the wide landscape of genres or the multitude of acting techniques—not to mention the actual range of their own abilities—they will be hard pressed to professionally serve the role in which they are cast. Now, this is a gross simplification of the vast and intricate complexities that go into honing the actor's craft. But, no matter how you cut it, awareness, inner and outer, is at the heart of acting.

And, you need to be aware of this!

PHYSICAL AWARENESS

The domain of bodywork in actor training is as deep and intricate as the human body itself. Honing the physical availability, sensitivity, flexibility, and responsiveness of the actor is paramount to artistic success in acting. The word "body" surely connotes a large spectrum of components. It encompasses all things cerebral, emotional, kinesthetic, muscular, neurological, sensory, and imaginative. All these parts of actor training are "housed" in the body. Actor training takes each of the areas separately and sets different developmental goals for each. Obviously, the miracle of the human body is as incredibly intricate and complicated as human behavior itself. It cannot be tackled in one general class. Yet, little by little, this infinitely complex instrument, which is both the "tool" and "material" with which an actor must sculpt their art, can be as finely tuned as a Stradivarius.

Speaking of musical instruments, I want you to now think of your own body as an instrument that must be played, like a musician plays a piano. Reflect for a moment how hard it is to play a piano, and it only has 88 keys! Ask yourself how many "keys" the human body and psyche have. Virtually an infinite number! Your body and psyche as instruments are exponentially more complicated than a piano. So, think how much more involved it is to play the human instrument. It gives you some perspective on what a Herculean challenge it is to not only train an actor, but become one…

SENSORY AWARENESS

The actor needs to be more sensitive to the world around them than the average person. The artistic challenges of recreating human behavior are so exacting that the actor needs to be hyper-receptive to their environs. How else will they be able to recreate a variety of different characters acting under the influence of an infinite number of given circumstances? Usually, beginning acting entails sensory exercises geared toward enhancing the five ways we have of receiving our world: sight, sound, taste, smell, and touch. Development of the five senses is integral to fine tuning the actor as an instrument. An actor who is insensitive to the world they live in and all its matrixes and nuances obviously won't be able to recreate it.

EXERCISE

Put the 5 senses in order of importance to you:

1.

2.

3.

4.

5.

Which of the five senses did you put as the most important? Why do you think this is so? Do you think this was always the case? Or have our senses evolved to match the world we live in?

"O WONDER! HOW MANY GOODLY CREATURES ARE THERE HERE! HOW BEAUTIOUS MANKIND IS! O BRAVE NEW WORLD, THAT HAS SUCH PEOPLE IN'T!"

- MIRANDA, *THE TEMPEST*, SHAKESPEARE

If you answered above that we are most reliant on our eyesight then you were correct. The principle way that we take in our world is by seeing it. Yet, do we really "see" all that we can see? And do we neglect other senses? Are we perhaps over-reliant on our sense of sight? For the most part people plow through life with their myopic vision blinders on, oblivious of much of what's going on around them. One of the quickest ways to verify this is by doing a simple partner "blind walk." Your teacher may instruct you in how to do this in class. If not, feel free to try it on your own. I am sure that you will find it "illuminating" and "eye opening"! (See the exercises listed at the end of this chapter.) After you are done and you "gain" your eyesight back, notice how much more aware you are of all that surrounds you.

Another way to test how much you really "see" what's around you is to ask yourself if you can properly identify—without now looking—the eye color of your best friend, or your teacher, or your roommates. How well do you really look at people? How well do you really "see" them? Could you have taken more time to really "see" them up to now? If you weren't really seeing them when you were interacting with them, then what *were* you doing?

By increasing our sensitivity to the world around us, it's almost as if we discover a whole "brave new world" out there. Try it.

YOUR WORLD AS A STAGE

The world around us is a constant source of unrelenting drama. There is no theatrical fiction that can match the daily conflicts that unfold in our lives, from the hysterical and unbelievable, to the tragic and sublimely beautiful. From the very beginning of this twisting and fascinating road of consciousness we call life to the bitter finale, we play dozens of roles and encounter an endless cast of amazing characters.

"ALL THE WORLD'S A STAGE AND ALL THE MEN AND WOMEN IN IT MERELY PLAYERS."

- Jacques, *As You Like It*, William Shakespeare

If this acting class does nothing more than highlight the tapestry of drama that already encompasses you and makes you more aware of the word around you then it has done its job. But perhaps you might choose to explore a little deeper and take a look at how you play your part in the universal drama. Perhaps you might want to take a look at all the characters you already naturally play over the course of this class. "All the men and women," that means *you*! But to do so you will have to increase your awareness of not only this orchestra called life, but tune your instrument to play along harmoniously.

EXERCISE

Answer the following questions:

The Slow-motion walk

Part 1:

- *Location:* Find a place away from your home neighborhood where the chances that you will run into anyone you know are slim to none. An ideal place would be in nature away from an urban environment, like the beach, or a secluded path in the woods. But if you live in a major metropolitan area and this is impossible try to find either a large park or quiet area of town.

- *Time:* 1 hour. Set aside 30 minutes to do the exercise and 30 minutes to write about it afterward.

- *Instructions:* Once you are in your selected location,

   - Turn off your mobile phones or any other electronic device that could possibly distract you.

   - Turn off your iPod. No music!

   - Begin to walk at a very, very, very slow pace, as if you were walking in slow-motion.

   - Continue walking this pace for the entire 30 minutes.

   - This must be done alone!

   - Notice what happens!

   - Enjoy the gift!

The Slow-motion walk

Part 2:

In the space below write what you noticed during your walk. What did slowing down do to you physically? Emotionally? Mentally?

Q Did you notice a change in your sensory awareness?

Q Did you feel the same at the end of it as you did during the beginning?

Q What did you notice about the world around you?

Q Be honest with yourself. Did you find that you actually completed the exercise as the directions stated or did you allow other factors (i.e. being distracted, uncommitted, self-conscious or embarrassment) keep you from successfully completing the exercise?

CHAPTER

EASE 15

> *"It is the lightness of touch which more than anything else makes an artist"*
>
> - EDWARD EGGLESTON

EASE

Acting, either in front of a live audience or in front of the camera tends to increase people's self-consciousness. Tension, both physical and emotional, is an immediate by product of increased self-consciousness. Much of actor training involves helping the actor relax the body and free up the mind in order to increase spontaneity, imagination, emotional availability, vocal range, physical adroitness and the actor's overall relation of artistic impulse to expression. Many acting techniques employ a variety of relaxation exercises all geared toward tension reduction. However, many actors don't even realize that they are tense while they are working. It is only after the fact, when they receive critiques of their work by directors and teachers that they are aware they were working with tension. The seminal Russian acting director and teacher, Konstantin Stanislavski, developed relaxation *études* that are still in use today. Many of them were picked up and elaborated on by Lee Strasberg at the famed Actor's Studio in New York City. However, Michael Chekhov, who was by Stanislavski's own admission "my most brilliant student", found a better way to work on stage than to seek relaxation *per se*. Chekhov realized that if he told his body to simply "move with *ease*" all tension went away. He discovered a new found lightness and freedom in his work by adding "the feeling of ease."

In much of contemporary American culture we are applauded for "hard" work and "muscling" or "powering" through things, as if somehow the amount of effort itself that it takes to do something should be rewarded for itself alone. Well, art is different, and all masterpieces have a sense of lightness and ease in them. The more masterful the artist the more ease and less effort they work with. One doesn't see the work in the work of a genius. Acting should be the same way. On stage we don't want to see an actor working hard to find a moment, we want to watch the character doing what she or he does, and nothing more.

Why make life more fraught with tension than it already is? Why make performing more stressful than it already is? Notice how much easier things become when you ask your body to work or play with the feeling of "ease".

THE FEELING OF EASE IS AN IMMEDIATE AND TANGIBLE METHOD TO REDUCE TENSION IN PERFORMANCE.

EXERCISE TO DO

I suggest you try this out for yourself. Whatever you are doing right now, even just reading, tell yourself to do it with the "feeling of ease." Stand up, sit down, walk around the room, pick up an object, answer the phone, open a beverage, brush your teeth, take notes in class, whatever, it doesn't' matter, but add to what you are doing the "feeling of ease". I guarantee you there will be a difference. Notice what happens and enjoy the gift!

CHAPTER

INCORPORATION 16

> *"The soul desires to dwell with the body*
> *because without the members of the body*
> *it can neither act nor feel."*
>
> - LEONARDO DA VINCI

INCORPORATION

The twentieth century Russian acting genius Michael Chekhov said that the actor training can be boiled down to the equation of "Concentration" + "Imagination" + "Incorporation" = "Inspiration."

Concentration, which we've talked about already, is pretty self-evident. So is the necessity of imagination for the actor, which we will address in the next chapter. Without these two things, it would be hard for an actor to do his or her job. But what do you think that Chekhov, a brilliantly talented actor in his own right, and a major star in his day in Russia, meant by "incorporation?"

Let's start again with a dictionary definition of "incorporation" and then take it from there.

DICTIONARY DEFINITION

in·cor·po·rate   P   Pronunciation Key (n-kôrp-rt)
v. **in·cor·po·rat·ed, in·cor·po·rat·ing, in·cor·po·rates**
v. tr.

- To unite (one thing) with something else already in existence: *incorporated the letter into her diary.*
- To admit as a member to a corporation or similar organization.
- To cause to merge or combine together into a united whole.
- To cause to form into a legal corporation: *incorporate a business.*
- To give substance or material form to; embody.
- *Linguistics.* To cause (a word, for example) to undergo noun incorporation.
  - *v. intr.*

- To become united or combined into an organized body.
- To become or form a legal corporation: *San Antonio incorporated as a city in 1837.*
- *Linguistics.* To be formed by or allow formation by noun incorporation.

Which part of the dictionary definition do you think Chekhov was referring to?

The Latin roots of incorporation are *in – corpus*, which literally means "in – body."

Again from the dictionary:

[Middle English incorporaten, from Late Latin incorporre, incorport-, *to form into a body:* Latin in-, *causative pref.*; see **in**-2 + Latin corpus, corpor-, *body*, **see corpus**.]

Christians will be familiar with this from church services via the expression *Corpus Christi*, which means the body of Christ.

What Michael Chekhov meant by this third step in the actor's process is that what exists in the imagination must be "given a body," must be "formed into a body." This is exactly what actors do: They "give body" to a dramatic fiction.

A play isn't real. It is a dramatic fiction composed of a series of words on a page. A guy named Hamlet who does all the stuff in the play of the same name doesn't really exist. There is no real person named Hamlet. Hamlet is a character, one who sprang from the deep well of the imagination of the playwright William Shakespeare. Until a production of Hamlet goes into rehearsal, it is just a collection of words on a page, albeit delectable ones! Until an actor is cast in the role of Hamlet, the words are a composite of literature. But, when an actor cast in the part of Hamlet takes to the stage in performance, the fiction literally is given life. It is given body by the actor, his concentration, his imagination, and ideally his inspiration!

This is why we keep saying that acting is doing. It involves your body, mind, and spirit. That is why you have to be present to do it. That is why you need to actively engage in the exercises in class. Because acting needs you to embody it!

 CONCENTRATION + IMAGINATION + INCORPORATION = INSPIRATION

EXERCISE

Answer the following questions:

Exercise TO DO: Here is a simple acting exercise that uses your imagination and forces you to completely focus on "doing." For actors it is necessary to believe in things that aren't really there. Actors must choose to believe for themselves what they are doing on stage. As the actor believes so does the audience. The following is a simple exercise that requires concentration and imagination. Take a small object (a pen, a rock, a notebook, a Chihuahua, anything around you) and pick it up and put it down. Repeat this several times, becoming more and more familiar with how the object feels in your hand each time: weight, size, texture, etc. Then repeat the same action, but this time without the real object. Rather in place of the real object pick up an imaginary version of the same thing using the exact same physical movement. Use your senses to feel it as if it were still in your hand. Do this several times, each time working for greater specificity for the visualization.

CHAPTER

IMAGINATION

17

"... an actor is exactly as big as his imagination."

- Minnie Maddern Fiske

CHILD'S PLAY

Do you realize that you already held the magic of acting in your hands? There actually was a time in your life when you played with it every day and did so brilliantly. It was part of the built-in luxury edition package that is your mind. At this time in your life the magic was unfettered, limitless and all-powerful. It was at your immediate beck and call; it needed no warming up. It took any shape you suggested and did it better than you initially imagined. It never failed you. Ever. It transported you to places you never thought you could go, and beyond.

This magical power is your imagination. It is the one essential ingredient to acting. The time in your life when you naturally used this priceless jewel was your childhood. The mind of a child is naturally open, accepting, limitless, inviting and curious. A young imagination welcomes fantastical images and does so without judgment. The more the merrier in fact. This, of course, was before parental, societal, religious, educational, and all the other behavioral constrictions devised by man, got a hold of it. These well-meaning institutions have eagerly worked to replace your beautiful child's imagination with ideas from that quintessentially mind-numbing manual: "How Things Are Supposed To Be Done The Right Way By Adult People Everywhere"! To quote my colleague at Cal State Long Beach, Dr. Joanne Gordon, were your imagination to read this manual it would cry out: "Boring! Boring!! Boring!!!"

A good friend of mine, Stephanie, is a French painter. At dinner one night in Paris she told me a story that illustrates the phenomenon of how the most well intentioned adults quite often squelch the imagination of young children. Stephanie has two young children, Emma and Matteo. They, like their mother, enjoy painting. Twice a week Stephanie volunteers at Emma's elementary school assisting the art teacher there. On one particular afternoon this teacher asked the pupils to draw a person. The class, full of young vital imaginations, sprung instantly to life. Pencils struck paper with gusto, verve and confidence. There was execution without hesitation or contemplation. There was no fear of doing it the wrong way. There was just the doing. The images appeared as if out of nowhere and a multitude of charcoal bodies came to life. Limbs were akimbo and out of proportion to torsos; composition was wild and irregular; shapes and sizes were bold and brash; the room was literally peopled with imaginary bodies. It was also filled with the atmosphere of joy that the act of creation brings with it. As Stephanie walked around the room she came across a girl drawing diligently in the corner. Stephanie was taken aback by what she saw. This girl's work was sure and strong, unique, idiosyncratic and somehow compelling, even for her young age. The lines were unbroken and fully stroked. The composition was balanced, whole and possessed a more mature asymmetry than one might expect. Everything Stephanie observed in this girl's work pointed to natural ability. From Stephanie's perspective, this young girl had artistic talent. As was to be expected the body had two legs, two arms, a torso, a neck, but…no head. After a while, the little girl put down her pencil, looked at what she had created and smiled up at Stephanie. This young artist's work, as she envisioned it, was done. Then the teacher arrived. After looking at the drawing for a few seconds the teacher said the to the student, "There's no head". The girl replied, "Yes, I know." The teacher continued, "But it can't be a person if there is no head." The artist in this young girl countered, "Well, this is how I see this particular person. I imagined a person without a head." The teacher having none of this said "It can't be a person if it doesn't have a head. People have heads. You need to learn how to draw heads if you are going to draw people. So, please, put a head on your person and finish it". With that, the teacher, assuming that she was helping the young student, walked away. The little girl stared at her drawing morosely for a minute or so and then peered sadly up at Stephanie. This teacher had just killed this girl's joy in the creative process. Evidently she must have done something wrong because the teacher said so. The young girl then reluctantly picked up her pencil to dutifully supply the missing head. Stephanie, incensed by this teacher's lack of imagination, placed her hand on the little girl's, took the pencil away from her, looked her in the eye and said, "Your person is beautiful just the way you drew it. Don't change a thing."

 IMAGINATION HAS RULES, BUT WE CAN ONLY GUESS WHAT THEY ARE.   – Mason Cooley

THE ACTOR'S IMAGINATION

An actor is artistically impotent without a facile, sharp and penetrating imagination. It is impossible to create a character without it. More than anything else, an actor's ability to imagine themselves in the shoes of the character is determined by the potency of their imagination.

 IMAGINATION IS THE ULTIMATE KEY TO ACTING.

If there is one key that can never be taken off an actor's proverbial key ring it is the key of imagination. What is acting but the free play of the imagination? Actors must be able to do both, imagine and play. As mentioned earlier, we all acted when we were children. We effortlessly flowed from one character to another. The range in our repertoire was enormous and included iconic and archetypal figures of all kinds. And we all played. It wasn't just "child's play" either, as if that is something to be discouraged anyway! Later on in life many an adult will try hard to replace the profound joy of "child's play" with money, material items and self-satisfying or self-reinforcing conventions. But deep down, we all know "Child's Play" is the dance of the divine inside us all. Actors not only know it, they must live it and let it live in them in their work.

Yet, there is always hope! Your imagination never goes away and will never leave you. It is only waiting for you to grasp it again, to make it the target of your artistic attention so that it too can grow and develop along with the other aspects of who you are. Part of the job of any acting class will be to help you get back to this pure place of blissful naiveté and boundless creativity, a place where we all once played naturally and freely as children.

DICTIONARY DEFINITION OF IMAGINATION

The dictionary defines the imagination as the following:

i·mag·i·na·tion
n.

- The formation of a mental image of something that is neither perceived as real nor present to the senses.

- The mental image so formed.

- The ability or tendency to form such images.

- The ability to confront and deal with reality by using the creative power of the mind; resourcefulness: *handled the problems with great imagination.*

- A traditional or widely held belief or opinion.

Source: *The American Heritage® Dictionary of the English Language, Fourth Edition*
Copyright © 2000 by Houghton Mifflin Company.
Published by Houghton Mifflin Company. All rights reserved.

What is the imagination but the part of our mind that deals in *images* and *pictures*? Recent scientific research in the fields of neuro-psychology, sports psychology and quantum mechanics postulate that much of how the mind works is through a series of images that are stimulated by electronic impulses passing along the vast network of synaptic connections in the brain. To imagine, that is to call up images, is the natural way of working for the mind.

For the sake of acting, I want you to think of images as a continuum from past through the present and into the future. Images from our past we call memory. Although we can play with them to some extent, for the most part they are unchanging. They may fade with time or shift a little, but we have a more or less fixed idea or picture of what they are as the way we remember them. Images of things that have yet to happen we call fantasy. This is the realm of the imagination, and hence, the actor. The ability to imagine that which we have yet to see is what we train in the actor, to see what others have yet to see. Characters in a play don't really exist. They are just words on a page. It is up the actor to literally imagine them into existence. The timeline of images moves from left to right across the page, from memory through the present and into fantasy.

PAST   **PRESENT MOMENT**   **FUTURE**

+ -------------→--------------→--→-------------→---------------- +

MEMORY = fixed images   **IMAGINATION = fluid images**

Fantasy is a freewheeling, non-stop, fluid association of images. When fantastical images come to us they are amalgamations of the known and the unknown, our waking state and dreams. Imagination springs out of the now into the future; although it might be informed by the past it comes not from memory. It is free of the shackles of the past.

HOW NOW, HORATIO? YOU TREMBLE AND LOOK PALE. IS NOT THIS SOMETHING MORE
THAN FANTASY?

- *HAMLET*, WILLIAM SHAKESPEARE

THE MAGIC IF...

One of the most important discoveries that the grandfather of modern actor training, Konstantin Stanislavksi, stumbled upon was that of the "magic if..." After years of trial and tribulation with his actors at the revered Moscow Art Theatre in Russia he came to the conclusion that his actors performed more naturally, that is to say moe realistically under imaginary circumstances when were acting "as if" they were the character instead of trying to believe that they "really are" the character. Everyone except the mentally ill person is aware, to a greater or lesser extent, who they are. Likewise, actors while performing a part never truly forget that they are acting, nor should they attempt to do so. No matter how lost in the moment an actor may be there still remains some part of their mind that is conscious of the artistic game they are playing. After all that's why actors in Shakespeare's time were called "Players" and why the text the actors speak is called a "Play". It's all play under imaginary circumstances. When you were a kid playing cowboys and Indians, or whatever imaginary game you played in your backyard, you never lost sight of the fact that you were playing. You acted "as if" you were the imaginary figure you wanted to be. And until your parents called you in for dinner you were that person in your imagination. The "as if" is the secret passageway into your imagination.

Therefore it can be said that the door into character begins with the words "as if..." An actor playing the coveted title role in Shakespeare's great tragedy "Macbeth" will never forget that he, under the layers of costume, makeup and imagination, that he is who he is in real life. Yet, for the duration of the play, he will act "as if" he were the most bloody and ambitious man in all of Scotland!

IS THIS A DAGGER WHICH I SEE BEFORE ME, THE HANDLE TOWARD MY HAND? COME, LET ME CLUTCH THEE. I HAVE THEE NOT, AND YET I SEE THEE STILL. ART THOU NOT, FATAL VISION, SENSIBLE TO FEELING AS TO SIGHT? OR ART THOU BUT A DAGGER OF THE MIND, A FALSE CREATION, PROCEEDING FROM THE HEAT-OPPRESSED BRAIN?

MACBETH - WILLIAM SHAKESPEARE

Try it out. It works. And not just for acting. Try playing your favorite sport "as if" you were one of the superstars in the field. Play golf "as if" you were Tiger Woods, tennis "as is" you were Venus Williams, etc. You will be amazed at what happens. Your game will get better. The imagination is more powerful than your mind can imagine. Imagine that!

INTUIT "OUT OF THE BOX"

Additionally, it is important to allow for the possibility of extraordinary impulses. We have all heard the phrase "think out of the box". What this means is that true creativity happens when we think beyond what is already known, outside of the usual paradigms and templates. It means taking the road less traveled in order to discover the road never before walked. This brings us back to our earlier discussion on conformity and individuality. To think or do anything "out of the box" you have to be willing to build on the established, discard it or reshape it somehow.

No less than the scientific genius Einstein professed that one needed to nurture what he called "possibility thinking"; he created a technique to do it called the "thought experiment" in which at the age of 16 he *imagined* chasing after a beam of light in order to examine its existence. Who had ever thought of chasing after a beam of light before Einstein? No one. And that's the point. Your average intellect might think that that's crazy. Well, a genius like Einstein didn't listen to the average intellect. He thought and *imagined* for himself; this imagining eventually lead him to his great hypothesis, the Theory of Relativity. Now, that's thinking out of the box! You have to give your ideas, imaginings and feelings full reign to run where they wish if you are to ever get out of the box.

NOT THAT WHICH IS INSPIRES THE CREATION, BUT THAT WHICH MAY BE; NOT THE ACTUAL, BUT THE POSSIBLE.

- RUDOLPH STEINER

Intuiting and imagining are two ways to "think" out of the box. One involves trusting your intuition, that inner innate "sense" that you have about something, "listening to it", as it were, and then going where it suggests, even if it makes no cerebral "sense" whatsoever! The other involves actively fantasizing and daydreaming, nurturing and projecting images onto the widest possible screen in your mind's eye, while giving them full reign to run as they wish, attempting not to control them in any fashion. In fact Einstein himself writes in his tome *Autobiographical Notes* that he used to visualize his work as a series of cinematic images that flowed from one into another. He preferred to allow his mind to run to images that had never existed before. And he was a scientist!

I believe the Russian acting genius Michael Chekhov said it most clearly:

"IMAGINE IT; SEE IT; BE IT!"

- MICHAEL CHEKHOV

This is what actors do. They imagine a character, see it clearly in their mind's eye, and finally "become" it by incorporating the image into their body. They then propel that character into the action of the given circumstances in order to satisfy the demands of the piece in which they are performing.

> *"O for a Muse of fire, that would ascend*
> *The brightest heaven of invention,*
> *A kingdom for a stage, princes to act*
> *And monarchs to behold the swelling scene!"*
>
> - Chorus, *Henry V*, William Shakespeare

O, FOR A MUSE...

Inspiration, there is no artistic or creative work without it. It is everything to the imaginative spirit. Inspiration in action is what separates the sublime from the pedestrian, the revelatory from the pedantic, the unique from the clichéd, and the authentic from the imitation.

Over two thousand years ago, when Greek gods still ruled nascent civilization from their lofty perch atop mount Olympus the nine Muses were the source of all inspiration. Each muse presided over a different aspect of the arts and sciences. They served as guiding spirits to those working in the respective faculties. During this mythological era, should a starving Greek artist have needed a little shot of inspiration, all they had to do was call on the appropriate Muse. These powerful Muses were the nine "go-to gals" when Hellenic artists and scientists needed a little protean boost. This is how the appellation "muse" came to be synonymous with a source of inspiration, and eventually how the word worked its way into our modern lexicon. Unfortunately for us, things in this realm have changed a bit over time. No longer can we, when feeling uninspired, just ring Zeus and ask his permission for an artistic date with any of his nine daughters!

"WHAT I MEAN BY THE MUSE IS THAT UNIMPEDED CLEARNESS OF THE INTUITIVE POWERS, WHICH A PERFECTLY TRUTHFUL ADHERENCE TO EVERY ADMONITION OF THE HIGHER INSTINCTS WOULD BRING TO A FINELY ORGANIZED HUMAN BEING.... SHOULD THESE FACULTIES HAVE FREE PLAY, I BELIEVE THEY WILL OPEN NEW, DEEPER AND PURER SOURCES OF JOYOUS INSPIRATION THAN HAVE YET REFRESHED THE EARTH."

- Margaret Fuller

Inspiration and muse are words that get tossed around a lot by artists, poets and theatre people. But what is it to truly be filled with said inspiration? Where can we find the muses of our time? And, frankly, what is inspiration exactly?

WHAT IS INSPIRATION?

When people speak of being inspired what they normally mean is that something has sparked in them a fire to create. Fanned properly that newfound flame fuels an individual's creation. Somehow, something somewhere fills that someone with the desire to make something new. This is called becoming inspired. When this someone is hit with this inspiration they are filled with the spirit of the act of creation. The spirit of this act has been blow into them, as it were; then it is the artist's responsibility to nurture that impulse to fruition, to carry it to term and give artistic birth to it, so to speak.

The American Heritage Dictionary defines inspiration as follows:

in·spi·ra·tion   P   Pronunciation Key   (nsp -r sh n)
n.

- Stimulation of the mind or emotions to a high level of feeling or activity.
- The condition of being so stimulated.
- An agency, such as a person or work of art, that moves the intellect or emotions or prompts action or invention.
- Something, such as a sudden creative act or idea, that is inspired.
- The quality of inspiring or exalting: *a painting full of inspiration.*
- Divine guidance or influence exerted directly on the mind and soul of humankind.
- The act of drawing in, especially the inhalation of air into the lungs.

Source: *The American Heritage® Dictionary of the English Language, Fourth Edition*
Copyright © 2000 by Houghton Mifflin Company.
Published by Houghton Mifflin Company. All rights reserved.

We can say that inspiration is an instrument of stimulation for the will, intellect or emotions in a creative endeavor. It is the motivator or provoking catalyst, the propulsion of the creative spirit. Or, said another way:

INSPIRATION IS THE ESSENTIAL IMPULSE TO ACTION IN A CREATIVE ACT. IT IS THE SPIRIT OF AN ARTISTIC GESTURE.

WHAT ARE THE SOURCES OF INSPIRATION?

A "source" is that from which we draw something. The million-dollar question then is: from what or where do we draw our inspiration if the nine muses are no longer to be found on Olympus? What are our modern, veritable sources of our inspiration? Why do some people seem more inspired than others?

For starters, if we were all inspired all the time then the world would be crowded with prodigious geniuses! Yet, we know from experience that this is certainly not the case, far from it. Inspiration, like the ocean, ebbs and flows. She is mercurial and capricious in nature. She sometimes strikes us when we least expect it and often eludes us when we most need her. Her sources are many and ever changing. Chasing inspiration can be like fishing for a wily minnow in the ocean. You will have a better chance with a net than a hook, and will succeed more often by attracting her rather than chasing after her.

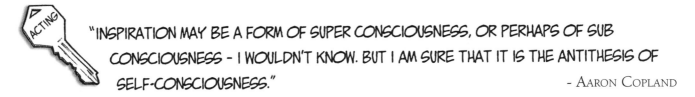

"INSPIRATION MAY BE A FORM OF SUPER CONSCIOUSNESS, OR PERHAPS OF SUB CONSCIOUSNESS - I WOULDN'T KNOW. BUT I AM SURE THAT IT IS THE ANTITHESIS OF SELF-CONSCIOUSNESS."

- AARON COPLAND

THE DATING GAME

In a way, divining inspiration is similar to dating. We rarely seek to date the person who is desperate to date us. Oddly enough we are often pulled toward people who show little or no attraction to us. To paraphrase Groucho Marx, we seemingly don't want to be a part of any club that will have us! The tantalizingly seductive and elusive Ms. Inspiration is the same way; she's the ultimate sleuth at detecting artistic desperation. One whiff of creative panic and she's gone with the wind. But, the artist who knows their own path, who has trust and confidence in "self" as well as their own technique…Ah! Now that's an artist that any of the nine puissant daughters of Zeus might want to date!

The creative stimulant called inspiration can be found in an endless number of sources. However, common ones include the imagination, people, ideas, music, art, texts, spirituality, love, and even nature. Frankly, there are an infinite number of sources and they can manifest themselves in any form that motivates an individual to artistic action. Just don't try too hard to find them! Rather create opportunities for them to reveal themselves to you. Make yourself more attractive to the muses by empowering yourself with a strong work ethic and efficacious technique. Just like in dating…the muses will then flock to you like bees to nectar!

BREATHE…

Of particular etymological interest is the fact that the word inspiration has its roots in the Latin meaning: "to breathe in". In other words, the genesis of the word inspiration is found in the biological act of breathing. As we are well aware, if not always conscious of, it is our breath that keeps us alive. Without it we would die in a matter of minutes. If you accept that life itself is the ultimate act of creativity then what breath does is fill us with its spirit. Breath keeps us in the game of creativity by constantly inhaling the elixir of life.

Conversely, we know that the word "expire" means to end or to die. The Latin etymology of this word is, expectedly, to "breath out". We speak colloquially that "time has expired" or that perishable food has an "expiration date". So, if we can say that life is the ultimate act of creation, and that breathing keeps us alive, then it is easy to see that the act of "inspiration" keeps us going. When we stop inspiring, we die. When we expire, the spirit has left us.

Metaphorically and literally, this is true for the artist as well. Artists strive to keep alive their inspiration or their creative spirit will expire. Therefore, the artist actively searches, or "breathes in", different sources in the hopes that they will become newly inspired. The acute reader will have noticed that in the previous list of sources many were external to the artist. In other words the artist had to "get" his or her inspiration from outside the self. They had to "breathe them in", metaphorically speaking.

At this point you can more clearly understand how vital passion, attention, concentration, awareness, listening, curiosity, human connection, risk and trust are to the creative soul. Each of these tools, properly honed and tuned, allows the actor a greater range of sensitivity and receptivity. It follows then that a greater availability of "self" affords a higher probability of being able to "breathe in" all potential sources of inspiration that are outside the "self". Actors who are more available, sensitive and receptive are, therefore, more inclined to snare the muse of inspiration in their artistic net.

INNER INSPIRATION

None of this of course precludes the possibility of tapping into an inner muse, that is, inspiration that comes from the "self". Quite often this is the case, as ideas, images and feelings can certainly originate from within. It takes a concentrated and sensitive "inner ear", however, to listen to these organic " inner voices". Our mental, psychological, physical and emotional habits, not to mention our mundane daily "business", are all enemies of inner inspiration. They happily and selfishly keep us distracted from the possibilities of new discoveries by chaining us to the post of familiarity.

This now returns us to our earlier discussion of the champion athlete and their singularity of mind and purpose. The fewer negative or "busy" thoughts we have during any particular day the more likely we are to keep focused on the target of our artistic attention. To do this we need to actively create opportunities for meditation, when we quiet our selves so that fresh, unexplored impulses can make themselves known to us. Albert Einstein, one of the most revolutionary, powerful and creative minds of the twentieth century used to wear the same color clothes every day so he didn't have to waste any thoughts on what to wear. He is also known for doing some of his best thinking while in the shower. Now that's economy of thought! He professed that in order to maximize your creative potential no moment in the day should be taken for granted. Steven Spielberg is similarly quoted as saying that some of his best ideas came to him while stuck in traffic on the highway. Too many of us can unfortunately relate to that. You don't have to go to a yoga class in order to meditate. There is no excuse for not establishing this reflective "mind-time" during your day. Creating quiet or reflective moments in the day, when you're not running around multi-tasking or doing a thousand and one things, is when you are most likely to experience flashes of inner inspiration. Actively seek them out! They will not coming looking for you. Purposefully create inviting moments in which to daydream and fantasize. These opportunities do not just magically appear. It is up to each individual artist and their own self-discipline to instigate them. The artist who is proactive mindfully fosters the revelation of inner inspiration.

"WHAT LIES BEHIND US, AND WHAT LIES BEFORE US ARE TINY MATTERS COMPARED TO WHAT LIES WITHIN US."

- RALPH WALDO EMERSON

TECHNIQUE AND INSPIRATION

If quality creative work depends on inspiration, and inspiration is hard to come by, it can then be concluded that the artist who is more often touched by inspiration has a greater chance of dynamic expression and multiple dimension in their work than one who isn't. Creating an attractive and accessible environment for inspiration is much of what actor training and technique is about. Actor training aims to develop repeatable and inviting working conditions in which to attract and catch artistic inspiration. It can't guarantee that actors will find inspiration each time they work. But it can provide them promising conditions in which to cast their artistic net and hopefully entrap fleeting inspiration. Technique allows the actor to steer a sure and steady course when the fickle muses escape the net and leave them sailing solo!

"GENIUS IS ONE PER CENT INSPIRATION, NINETY-NINE PER CENT PERSPIRATION"

- THOMAS ALVA EDISON

And none of this ever happens without hard work, years of dedication and discipline. Thomas Edison's wise words bear heeding. Only hard work and thoughtful effort will lead to inspiration. One of my first acting teachers, Jack Clay always said to us in his class:

"IT TAKES TWENTY YEARS TO BECOME AN ACTOR."

- JACK CLAY

As a young thespian beginning my training I was reluctant to believe this. As an actor who now works from the other side of those twenty years, I can see that Jack was right. Twenty years is indeed what it takes; in fact, it is only the beginning. It is not that a young actor can't find immediate success, most likely in television or film, the two mediums that are more likely to support and propel an untested neophyte into the raging stratosphere of fame and fortune. Of course "overnight" success can and does occasionally happen. Yet, usually many years of hard work and perseverance have gone into the "overnight" discovery of this "new" actor. What the necessary two-decade benchmark truly implies is that the human experience and accessibility that a career in acting requires can only be acquired over time. In a sense, an actor's ability can be compared to a sophisticated Côtes du Rhône wine. Of course, you can drink this classic French vintage when it's young, but a Châteauneuf du Pape will taste infinitely better when it has had time to mature and reveal its complexities! Likewise, a young actor may come up with the occasional inspired performance, but it is the seasoned actor who can find them with greater precision and ease as well as more regularity and repeatability.

In order to endure twenty years as an actor you will have to "out-perspire" the competition around you. However, if you find you have the psychological tenacity, you can't imagine doing anything else with your life, you feel a deep inner pull to express yourself through human behavior and imagination, and you are willing to take the time and patience that is needed to develop the skills of acting, then perhaps you will have stumbled into a life's work as an actor. There can be no greater discover than that of a life's work. For once you have it you have a compass for how to live your life. You may go off course from time to time but you will be able to recognize that you are off course; consequently, you will never be lost and can set yourself straight again. If this discovery of your *raison d'être* happens to be for acting then you will be handed another gift, that of a vocation. A vocation is something that one is called to do. An occupation on the other hand is a job one does to earn money. Rarely do they overlap. Lucky is the soul who discovers their "calling" in life and can make a living at it.

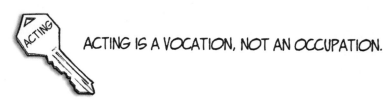 ACTING IS A VOCATION, NOT AN OCCUPATION.

EXERCISE

Answer the following questions:

Q Write down five things, people or events that are a source of inspiration for you in your life.

CHAPTER

STAGE FRIGHT

19

> *"The only thing we have to fear is fear itself."*
>
> - FRANKLIN D. ROOSEVELT

STAGE FRIGHT

Have you ever wondered why when you get up in front of a lot of people all of a sudden you feel a little nervous, or perhaps even worse, downright scared? Moments before as you chat amiably in the wings you feel fine and quite relaxed. Then you walk on stage and look out over the audience; you see hundreds of pairs of eyes staring at you. All at you! You've never seen such a strange sight. Then something happens. Your heart starts to pound, your stomach gets the "butterflies," and the lights blind your eyes because your pupils are swelling. Your palms are sweating enough to fill the Hoover dam, and yet your mouth is completely dry. The silence is deafening, and all you can hear is your heart pounding on your drums like a rabid Banshee. One single second on stage seems to last an eternity; it's as if time itself has downshifted into slow motion. It feels like you're on sensory overload. The experience is almost paralyzing. What the hell is happening?!

This is the moment that either sucks people into acting like a drug or drives them away from it forever. It is the magic of the stage. The power is bewitching, yet its sorcery is not for everyone. It is a place where only the courageous dare tread. But once you're bitten, the habit is addicting. And it's a hard one to kick.

Now if you have never experienced this pseudo-hallucinatory high in front of a large group of people, you are in the minority. Chances are most of you reading this book at some time or another experienced this mind and body-altering phenomenon. The body's reaction to the heightened pressure of performing in front of a large number of people is often called "stage fright." Commonly, this fear is referred to as "nerves" or getting the "butterflies" because it feels as if a thousand butterflies are fluttering away in your stomach. It comes in many different varieties—it can be light or it can be paralyzing. Your ability to handle these delicately winged creatures will determine whether or not you'll be able to take flight as an actor.

WHAT IS STAGE FRIGHT ACTUALLY?

When the body and mind are put under stress they both react accordingly. Literally, getting stage fright is an endorphin rush, similar to a "runner's high." This is why all the body's senses are heightened. Just standing up and saying your name in front of a group of people can be stressful to some people. It is totally natural to feel at least a bit nervous in front of a crowd; like I've said, almost everyone does. You're not alone. I've yet to meet an actor, professional or amateur, who doesn't get a least a little "twang" in their guts on opening night. However, some people get more scared than others. If in the course of this acting class you are asked to get up and do an exercise in front of all your classmates, you might feel this twang too. Not to worry. It's a normal reaction to stress. Let's take a look.

What is it about getting up in front of others that makes us all feel that funky twang? The "butterflies," "nerves," or "stage fright" is to one degree or another a universally human reaction. You will find it in almost all peoples from every society across the planet. It is the body's way of taking care of itself under high-pressure situations. This is true in acting because being on stage is literally stressful. That is to say, it is not a natural state of being. One could say it is an artificial reality. It is a state of heightened behavior. Simply put, being on stage is physically and mentally more stressful than being off stage. The body and mind have to cope with this shift somehow; so, they shift into a higher gear. The stage reality demands more energy then just everyday existing. It demands more mental acuity, more oxygen, more physical agility, more awareness, more sensitivity, quicker reaction times, etc.

When the human body is forced out of more natural situations it shifts into "stress mode." In the right measure this "stress mode" is actually a good thing. Look at it this way, it also means you care. If you didn't care, you wouldn't get nervous! We'll come back to this caring aspect in a bit.

 STAGE FRIGHT IS THE BODY'S NATURAL WAY OF COPING WITH THE STRESS OF BEING ON STAGE. BREATHING SLOWLY HELPS REGULATE THE BODY'S REACTIONS.

Now, although much is made of living a stress-free life, it is worth noting that not all forms of stress are alike.

STRESS

There is a difference between stress that enhances performance and stress that debilitates it. When you hear people talk of stress reduction, what is really meant is that we desire to reduce the debilitating stress in our lives. Debilitating stress is that which inhibits our performance of whatever task is at hand. On the flip side, what we want to encourage, and what much of actor training is about, is maximizing performance ability under conditions of desirable stress.

Yes, stress can actually be a desirable thing! Ask yourself this: Do you think it is stressful playing in the Super Bowl of football, the Word Series of baseball, the U.S. Open of golf or the final of soccer's World Cup? You bet it's stressful! But doesn't every champion athlete desire to be in the final? Doesn't every Olympic athlete train from the time they were young to be in the gold medal match with the whole world watching? Of course they do! Athletes desire to be "center court"; they seek the positive stress that comes with competition at the world-class level. Actors seek a similar form of positive stress, being "center stage."

Ever notice that you actually perform better when you are under a little pressure? When you have a paper due or a test coming up? There is actually a bio-psychological reason for this. The body and mind perform better when under pressure because over tens of thousands of years of evolution it meant the difference between life and death. It meant either going hunting or being the hunted. In a word, it meant survival. Nowadays, obviously, the stakes are not as high, or at least not often. They might be if you find yourself in a combat situation while in the armed services or the police force. But for most of us life or death situations rarely, if ever, present themselves. This is one of the true benefits of modernity! Yet, the phenomenon of becoming nervous has its genetic roots in our evolutionary history. Of course, the trick is to monitor this heightened state and not to let the pressure debilitate your performance during times of desirable stress. But stress properly handled helps us perform above our normal everyday capacity. Let's take a look at why this is.

THE BUTTERFLIES

Stress, in a fashion, is a type of pain. And pain is the body's way of alerting the mind to a potentially dangerous situation. When the mind in conjunction with the central nervous system senses a dangerous or stressful situation, it orders the circulatory system to send more blood, and hence more oxygen, to where it is most needed. Endorphin levels are also immediately increased, causing a boost in mood and energy. Endorphins, as you may remember from your biology class, are opiate proteins found in the brain with pain-relieving properties. They help the body deal with "pain," perceived or real, by increasing a natural form of morphine, which elevates mood and reduces pain. All stressful situations demand the mind to think faster and with greater consequences than normal situations. Hence, the brain demands more oxygen and higher energy levels from the rest of the body to do this. In times of stress the autonomic nervous system instinctively draws blood away from the areas of the body where it is less needed and sends it to those where it is actively needed. For example, in times of high pressure, it is rare that digestion is of prime importance. A Coney Island hot dog-eating contest might be the rare exception to this case!

What you are actually feeling when you get the "butterflies" is blood flowing out of the intestinal region and to the brain. It can then be said that the "butterflies" are a good thing! They are your body helping you deal more efficiently with stress by sending oxygen where it is needed most.

Although a minute portion of people might say that being on stage is literally painful, the overwhelming majority, I suspect, would categorize it as the brain does, as a "perceived" pain. In other words, your body doesn't know that it's not an actual pain. Yet it perceives the stress of going on stage as such. The body can't actually tell the difference, even if your brain can. Not taking any chances—a residual survival instinct—the body kicks into "dealing with pain mode." This is why simultaneously, and seemingly paradoxically, being on stage is both painful and pleasurable. It is also why physiologically it can literally be addicting, because it can be an endorphin high.

ETHICAL BUTTERFLIES

Additionally, but of equal importance, as I briefly mentioned before, you get the butterflies because you care about what you are doing. Caring about what you do is obviously a characteristic to be engendered. It is your inner ethical barometer telling you that this thing you're doing is important, has value, and needs to be nurtured properly. The butterflies therefore are also an ethical reaction to the task at hand. You instinctively know that it is "right" to care about what you are doing and to do a good job. If you didn't care, chances are you wouldn't get nervous.

In conclusion, it can be said that a healthy amount of "nerves" is desirable on two levels, biological and ethical. Finding the optimum balance of "nerves" or "butterflies" is another aspect of actor training. Acting technique gives actors the tools they need to channel their "energy" under stressful conditions in a productive direction to best articulate the work they care about.

So, now that you know literally what "stage fright" is, what does it all mean? It means the following:

 FEEL THE FEAR AND DO IT ANYWAY!

CHAPTER

"It is not because things are difficult that we do not dare; it is because we do no dare that they are difficult."

\- Lucius Annaeus Seneca

CONFIDENCE

Acting requires huge amounts of confidence. Confidence is, by definition, trust in yourself or others. It is sureness in your ability to successfully demonstrate a particular task or achieve a specific goal. Confidence comes from preparation and not by accident. Therefore, the better prepared you are to act, the more confident you will be once you get on stage. Preparation involves not only the work on one specific role but long-term training as well. If an actor is well trained they will be much more confident on stage than one who is untrained. Now, this may seem obvious, but you'd be surprised how under-prepared people are all the time in all aspects of life. Ask yourself how often you yourself are unprepared for class assignments, tests, or exams. I can tell you right now, you never want to go on stage under-prepared. Yet, if an actor happens to be under-prepared, they only have themselves to blame for the terror in which they find themselves.

You've probably heard the old adage, "an ounce of preparation is worth a pound of cure." Well, it's true. And if I told you that for every ounce of preparation you would reduce a corresponding "pound" of stage fright, would you prepare more? I bet you would! So, do it. Prepare. Confidence will flow from your preparation. I guarantee it.

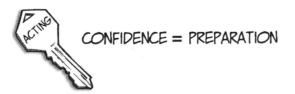 CONFIDENCE = PREPARATION

CONFIDENCE VS. COCKINESS

This is a secondary observation, but one worth mentioning. Confidence should not be confused with cockiness. Cockiness is *acting* like you are confident for the benefit of those around you. Confidence is for you and you alone; cockiness is for an audience of friends, family, peers, etc. Always strive for confidence in your work over the more superficial cockiness. Those who are confident don't need to act like it, because they already are confident. It is the cocky person who is ultimately fueled by insecurity. They feel the need to *show* the world that they are confident. If you need to show you're confident, you aren't. If you are it, you are it, and therefore have no need to demonstrate it. And deep down, we all know this…and can see the difference in others a mile away.

 WALK THE WALK; DON'T TALK THE TALK...

CHAPTER
TALENT 21

> *"…Talent is like electricity. We don't understand electricity. We use it!"*
>
> - MAYA ANGELOU

RELATIVE TALENT

You may have noticed that this far into a book on acting I have spent almost no time talking about talent. There is a very good reason for this. Talent is both subjective and innate. You are either born with an affinity to create character or you're not. Someone else either thinks you're talented or they don't. Consequently, there is not much you can do about it. Ultimately, it's relative anyway. Why spend time and energy focusing on something that is totally out of your control? It's a sad waste of both valuable commodities.

"THE MERE MECHANICAL TECHNIQUE OF ACTING CAN BE TAUGHT, BUT THE SPIRIT THAT IS TO GIVE LIFE TO LIFELESS FORMS MUST BE BORN IN A MAN. NO DRAMATIC COLLEGE CAN TEACH ITS PUPILS TO THINK OR TO FEEL. IT IS NATURE WHO MAKES OUR ARTISTS FOR US, THOUGH IT MAY BE ART WHO TAUGHT THEM THEIR RIGHT MODE OF EXPRESSION."

- OSCAR WILDE

TRUE TALENT

True talent is recognizing what abilities you do have and making the most of them. Both the recognizing and the making require your attention. What you *can* do about whatever level of relative talent you may be born with is apply yourself to the work with every ounce and fiber of your being. This is true talent. This is not out of your control. This is something you can *do*.

What you actually *can* do is be the most prepared person in the class, thereby boosting your confidence and your chances of performing better. What you *can* do is "out work" everyone else, or at least ensure that no one else is "outworking" you. Again, these things you *can* actually *do*. I promise if you do them it will make a difference, in any field of study. Talent for success is not an accident. If you don't work harder than those around you, chances are success will elude you. Deal with those aspects of the work that are within your control and let go of those that aren't. How much relative talent you have is not in your control; what you do with what talent you do have, is. Focus your attention on that.

 "TALENT IS NOTHING MORE THAN A PROLONGED PERIOD OF ATTENTION AND A SHORTENED PERIOD OF MENTAL ASSIMILATION."

– KONSTANTIN STANISLAVSKY

CHAPTER

THE ARTISTIC PARADOX: EGO VS. GENEROSITY

22

> *"Yes; the public is wonderfully tolerant.*
> *It forgives everything except genius."*
>
> - OSCAR WILDE

EGO

What acting—and any art form—asks of you is that you think, feel, and create from yourself, for yourself. Crudely put, art is an individual's expression or impression of the world they live in. This may seem egotistical; however, ultimately, it's not. It is historical truth that many artists have had enormous egos. Look at the legendary self-aggrandizement and self-promotion of Mark Twain, Oscar Wilde, Bernard Shaw, Pablo Picasso, Frank Sinatra, Elvis Presley, or even, more recently, Bono of U2 or the rap artist, Eminem. It takes a healthy ego and a lot of guts to get up in front of a stadium full of people and sing a song you wrote, or show your artwork at a gallery opening, or publish a novel for the entire world to read. This is so because inherent in the artistic act is a fair amount of personal vulnerability. It takes boatloads of tenacity, steely resolve, and thick skin to proverbially "put yourself out there." It's easy to be an artist when everyone loves your work. But it takes a giant portion of self-confidence to express how you see the world—which is what artists do—in the face of criticism, or even worse, flat-out rejection. But as with most things in life, it's all about finding the balance between what's enough ego and what's too much. That balance will only be found in the doing. Again, just do it. Just do the work. The work will reveal your talent. This resulting work, if an honest expression and extension of your creative individuality, will be a gift to those who receive it.

So, once more, you ask, "What does this have to do with me and this acting class?" I say to you, it has everything to do with you. If you took this class to sit back and listen to another lecture, you are in for a big surprise. Your instructor will demand of you commitment (there's that word again), bold action, and vigorous imagination over the course of this class. Acting will challenge you to reflect sincerely upon yourself and what you want to say. It will ask you to take a stand, believe in something, make choices, and take action. It is not important whether your teacher or any of your fellow classmates agree with your position or not. All that does matter is that you have something to say and stand up for it. That takes constructive ego. We will want to hear your opinions on your classmate's work, on the performances you will go to see, in the papers you write, and the group projects you create together.

Let's recall here one of the earlier keys of acting, as it is applicable here:

 HOW YOU TALK ABOUT YOUR WORK IS HOW YOUR WORK WILL BE.

If you don't' believe in your work, why should anyone else? No matter the métier, to cut against the grain of society, to tell the truth in the face of strong adversity demands an intrepid ego, a higher ego. Paradoxically, however, the purist artistic gesture, while perhaps initially forged in the crucible of ego, eventually reveals itself as a generous gift. Never forget that the truest artistic gesture is an offering of generosity to the world. Generosity will demand use of your higher ego, the creative and positive side of your ego, not the selfish ego.

THE HIGHER EGO

There are different types of egos. Without delving into the multitude of philosophical and psychological theories that address the subject of ego, it will suffice for our purposes to deal only with what the Russian acting genius Michael Chekhov called the "higher ego." Chekhov got this term from the German moral philosopher Rudolph Steiner. What Steiner and Chekhov meant by this higher ego is that there is a difference between an individual's creative (higher) ego and their everyday (lower) ego. For Chekhov the higher ego, or the artistic ego, is part of your creative idiosyncrasy. It is part of the unique spark that makes you, you. It is a spiritual well of artistic freedom and confidence that is to be cherished. It is not, however, the lower, quotidian ego that you take to the grocery store when you go shopping. The higher ego demands more focus, concentration, ease, attention, and respect. It is the precious and priceless potentiality that dwells in us all. It is that tethered belief that what you have to say is indeed worth saying and, more importantly, worth being heard. But it is fragile and needs to be nurtured with care and attention.

This higher ego should not to be confused with the seminal psychologist Sigmund Freud's triumvirate nomenclature of id, ego, and super ego. Although if one were to make comparisons, the lower ego that Chekhov refers to would be closely aligned with Freud's id and ego; and Chekhov's higher ego, the one we are interested in, would be matched with Freud's super ego, which has intrinsic moral and aesthetic value attached to its core.

Nor is Chekhov's higher ego to be confused with plain old self-absorbed egotism. Egotistical people care first and foremost about themselves, not the world around them. They are selfish and tend to be endlessly self-involved and therefore severely handicapped by their own limited capacity of love of self. Their boundaries of curiosity are alarmingly small. Therefore, so are they. Egotism gets pretty boring and predictable fairly quickly, for everyone involved. This sense of the word ego is anathema to Chekhov's higher ego.

When you come to this acting class, we look for you to bring with you the higher ego. Feel free to leave the others at home…

THE LEGACY OF YOU

 THE MEASURE OF ANY SOCIETY IS THE ART IT LEAVES BEHIND.

What do you plan on leaving behind? Have you ever thought about this? Most of the time in our consumer-driven society we think about what we can "get" out of everything. "What's in this for *me*?" is a ubiquitous phrase these days. Well, I ask you, what happens if you turn the phrase on its head? Ask instead, "What's in it for everyone around me?" "What does everyone else get *from me*?" That begs the question, "What's so great about me?" Seriously, I mean it. Examine for a while what is great about you. Once you figure this out then celebrate it through a healthy artistic means of expression.

What are you going to leave this class, your classmates, your professor, this university, your family, your friends, and this world with when you are done? What will they leave with from you? Poets leave their poems; painters leave their paintings; writers leave their writing; musicians leave their music; actors leave their performances. Seriously, think about it. What are you going to leave? What will be the legacy that is you?

Don't forget the generosity portion of the artistic paradox. Never forget that the truest artistic gesture is an offering of generosity from a creative individual to the world in which they live.

GENEROSITY

Generosity is the act of giving to others. "Give and you shall receive," as the old saying goes. This is what art, and therefore acting, is all about. There is no performance for the actor without an audience. It's no fun to act if there is no one there to act for.

 IT MATTERS MORE HOW ONE GIVES THAN WHAT ONE GIVES.

- Pierre Corneille

Let's take a closer look at what we mean by artistic generosity by considering the Spanish painter Pablo Picasso. His ego and womanizing are both legendary. But what a better place this world is for the artwork he left behind. Let's take his antiwar masterpiece *Guernica* as an illustration of the artistic paradox. It took a lifetime in the creating and thousands of previous paintings before it revealed itself to this genius painter almost instantaneously. Picasso's inspiration for this painting came to him as a reaction to unprecedented horrors perpetrated on behalf of the then dictator of Spain Francisco Franco against the civilian population. On April 27th, 1937, Hitler's growing war machine pounded the little Basque village in northern Spain of Guernica with incendiary bombs for over three hours. The townspeople of Guernica were instantly blazed to ashes as they ran from the raging inferno. This tiny town would go on to burn for three whole days, and close to sixteen hundred civilians were killed or wounded by Hitler's savage target practice.

When the news of the massacre in his native land rippled across Picasso's adopted home of Paris, France, millions took to the streets in protest. Yet he, the much misunderstood and revered artist of his time, fled immediately to his studio in order to express his outrage and horror at the killings. How he felt and thought at the time manifested on his canvas. But had the years of toil and exacting execution of technique not already been in his scabbard, the creative sword of inspiration drawn from it would not have had such haunting potency.

Although this painting has long been considered a masterpiece, it was not received as such when it was first revealed at the 1937 Paris Exhibition. In fact, quite to the contrary, it was ridiculed by much of the art press as a piece of junk that could have been doodled by an incoherent four-year-old child. It is important to keep in mind that even at this time Picasso was an extremely famous and successful artist who was hugely respected by art critiques worldwide. Yet like all geniuses, he was ahead of his time. Because Picasso held true and fast to his own artistic course, we are blessed with this colossal and visionary indictment of war.

This compelling reminder of human brutality is now housed in the venerable Reina Sofía, Spain's national museum of modern art. For many years it toured the world out of its temporary home, the museum of modern art in New York City. As a symbolic and powerful gesture, Picasso himself forbade the painting to enter Spain until the people of that country were free of Franco's cruel reign. Picasso died in 1973, and Franco soon after in 1975. Exactly one hundred years to the day of Picasso's birth, Spain took its place alongside other modern democracies and this iconic painting was welcomed to its rightful resting place on Spanish soil. *Guernica* now hangs as a resonant and artistically generous gift to the people of Spain from their native son, the most influential artist of the twentieth century, Pablo Picasso, a man of a substantive, yet higher, ego.

ONE CANNOT TRULY JUDGE A PIECE OF ART WITHOUT FULLY UNDERSTANDING THE PERSPECTIVE AND INTENTION OF THE ARTIST WHO CREATED IT. TO DO SO WOULD BE TO INCORRECTLY JUDGE FROM A PLACE OF IGNORANCE AND MYOPIA.

Image from Erich Lessing/Art Resource, NY

EXERCISE

Answer the following questions:

Exercise: Think about an art form you believe is important. It can be any form including, but not limited to, painting, drawing, music, theatre, sculpture, etc. Anything you believe is art. Write down why you feel this form of creative expression is important not only for the artist but for the individuals it eventually touches. Also include why you think this art changes people for the better.

PART

WORK ON
THE ROLE

II

CHAPTER

ACTING DEFINED 23

O, what a rogue and peasant slave am I!
Is it not monstrous that this player here,
But in a fiction, in a dream of passion,
Could force his soul so to his own conceit
That from her working all his visage wann'd,
Tears in his eyes, distraction in's aspect,
A broken voice, and his whole function suiting
With forms to his conceit? and all for nothing!
For Hecuba!

- WILLIAM SHAKESPEARE-*HAMLET*

YOUR DEFINITION OF ACTING

Even more than 400 years after Shakespeare wrote these words, Hamlet's amazement at the craft of acting is pretty spot on, wouldn't you say? As many of you may have had no exposure to Shakespeare, if you had trouble deciphering what Hamlet was saying about actors, ask your professor to clarify. It's rather extraordinary. When you think about it, what actors do is truly astonishing. But what is acting really? Can you define it? Can you describe what it is *exactly* that actors actually do? Before we go any further, use the space provided to write your thoughts on acting. You don't need to look ahead in the book or ask anyone else. You do need, however, to trust yourself. Remember the chapter on trust? This is not about getting it right. What we want to do is see what you think acting is now and then compare it with what you think it is at the end of the semester. This will highlight for you your preconceived notions about acting; they will then serve as a benchmark for how much you will grow during this class. Remember, there is no right or wrong here. So, run boldly into possible failure by writing your definition!

EXERCISE

Write your definition of acting:

EXERCISE

List the names of a few actors you admire and why you admire them:

THE DICTIONARY DEFINITION OF ACTING

Good. Now let's take a look at what the dictionary says acting is. The online dictionary www.dictionary.com defines acting the following way:

v. **act·ed, act·ing, acts**

v. tr.

- To play the part of; assume the dramatic role of: *She plans to act Lady Macbeth in summer stock.*
- To perform (a role) on the stage: *Act the part of the villain.*
  - To behave like or pose as; impersonate: *Don't act the fool.*
  - To behave in a manner suitable for: *Act your age.*

v. intr.

- To behave or comport oneself: *She acts like a born leader.*
- To perform in a dramatic role or roles.
- To be suitable for theatrical performance: *This scene acts well.*
- To behave affectedly or unnaturally; pretend.
- To appear or seem to be: *The dog acted ferocious.*
- To carry out an action: *We acted immediately. The governor has not yet acted on the bill.*
- To operate or function in a specific way: *His mind acts quickly.*
- To serve or function as a substitute for another: *A coin can act as a screwdriver.*
- To produce an effect: *waited five minutes for the anesthetic to act.*

Phrasal Verbs:

act out

- To perform in or as if in a play; represent dramatically: act out a story.
- To realize in action: wanted to act out his theory.
- To express (unconscious impulses, for example) in an overt manner without conscious understanding or regard for social appropriateness.

This is a little dry, don't you think?

THE ENCYCLOPEDIA DEFINITION OF ACTING

The online encyclopedia, Wikipedia, takes the dictionary definition into much more detail:

Acting is the work of an actor, a person in theatre, film, or any other storytelling medium who tells the story by portraying a character and, usually, speaking or singing the written text or play. From the Latin word agere meaning "to do," this is precisely what acting is. In acting, an actor suppresses or augments aspects of their personality in order to reveal the actions and motivations of the character for particular moments in time. The actor is said to be "assuming the role" of another, usually for the benefit of an audience, but also because it can bring one a sense of artistic satisfaction.

Actors are generally expected to possess a number of skills, including good vocal projection, clarity of speech, physical expressiveness, a good sense of perspective, emotional availability, a well developed imagination, the ability to analyze and understand dramatic text, and the ability to emulate or generate emotional and physical conditions. Well-rounded actors are often also skilled in singing, dancing, imitating dialects and accents, improvisation, observation and emulation, mime, stage combat, and performing classical texts such as Shakespeare. Many actors train at length in special programs or colleges to develop these skills, which have a wide range of different artistic philosophies and processes.

Modern pioneers in the area of acting have included Konstantin Stanislavski, Jerzy Grotowski, Lee Strasberg, Uta Hagen, Stella Adler, Eric Morris, Michael Chekhov, Viola Spolin, and Sanford Meisner.

For history and other details, see actor.

This seems pretty clear, doesn't it? But it is a little long winded…

OUR WORKING DEFINITION OF ACTING

Now we come to a more cogent and practical definition of acting; let's narrow the previous definitions down even further. For the purposes of this class, we will define acting as the following:

ACTING IS LIVING BELEIVABLY UNDER IMAGINARY CIRCUMSTANCES WITH PRECISE REPEATABILITY AND COMPLETE SPONTENEITY.

Memorize this. We will come back to it throughout the entire semester and talk later on about each component of the definition. But for now it is only important that you get a handle on the overall definition.

This definition is all well and good you might say, but what *does* an actor actually *do* to *do* this?

ACTING IS DOING

No matter whose definition of acting we use, we have to acknowledge that they all share one common element, the tenet that acting is *doing*.

One of the great American acting teachers of the twentieth century, Mr. Sanford Meisner, said that:

THE FOUNDATION OF ACTING IS THE REALITY OF DOING.

And what he meant by this is that when an actor steps on stage they must be actively engaged in *DOING* something, not necessarily FEELING something, although feelings do come along as part and parcel of the doing.

Another fabulous American acting teacher, Tony Barr in his classic tome *Acting for the Camera*, takes Meisner's definition a step further. Barr says that an actor actually DOES the following:

ACTING IS RESPONDING TO STIMULI IN IMAGINED CIRCUMSTANCES IN AN IMAGINATIVE, DYNAMIC MANNER THAT IS STYLISTICALLY TRUTHFUL TO THE CHARACTER AND HIS ENVIRONMENT SO AS TO COMMUNICATE EMOTIONS AND IDEAS TO AN AUDIENCE.

You should memorize Tony Barr's definition too.

In the following chapters, we'll take a look at each of the components of our working definition of acting, which again is,

ACTING IS LIVING BELEIVABLY UNDER IMAGINARY CIRCUMSTANCES WITH PRECISE REPEATABILITY AND COMPLETE SPONTENEITY.

EXERCISE

Answer the following questions:

Q How is this working definition different from yours?

CHAPTER 24

LIVING BELIEVABLY

"Acting? Oh, that's easy.
Just don't get caught doing it..."

\- SPENCER TRACEY

LIVING BELIEVABLY

What do you think is meant exactly by "living believably," and why is it important? Why is the definition of acting not "performing believably...?" After all, the actors are literally giving a performance, aren't they? True, most people do think of acting as performing, and in a very basic and obvious sense it is. A show put on in an edifice called a theatre in front of an audience is indeed called a performance. It only makes sense that what the actors are doing then is "performing." Right?

Well, sort of. As you have read this far you now understand that there is much more to acting than what meets the eye. In fact, if the audience is aware that an actor is "performing" while they are watching, then arguably the actor is not doing their job. That said, sometimes the style of the writing or direction purposely draws attention to the performance aspect of the actor's work, like in the case of plays by Bertolt Brecht and his Epic Theatre style of acting. But such highly stylized productions are more the exception than the rule. For the most part what you see on stage, on television, and in film is a theatrical style known as "Psychological Realism." In this ubiquitous form the artistic mandate is the verisimilitude of life. So, if the audience is consciously and actively aware of the actor's performance while watching then they are being distracted from the world of fiction that the actors are trying to create. What the actors in this case are doing is drawing attention to themselves at the expense of the play. This is self-defeating since what the actors are supposed to do is make the events of the play happen so that the story is told. Remember one of our initial premises that actors are first and foremost storytellers? Actors successfully achieve full immersion in the fiction of the story by "living" in the roles, not "performing" them. Only this truthful immersion into the character, of living, leads to a satisfactory artistic embodiment of the role for the actor, and consequently a thematic revelation of the entire dramatic piece for the audience.

THE INNER SENSE OF TRUTH

The grandfather of modern actor training, the Russian actor, director, and theorist, Konstantin Stanislavski, said that actors must develop an acute "inner sense of truth." When this is honed to a razor-sharp edge then the actor's experience in his imagination on stage is perfectly aligned with what the audience experiences in their seats. There is no disconnect between actor and audience when the acting is full of this inner truth. Ideally, the actor serves as a talisman or sherpa to transport the audience into the playwright's imagination. This cannot happen if the actor is concerned with his everyday self or his lower-egocentric ego. There must be what the great Polish director and acting theorist Jerzy Grotowski called a "self-immolation" on the actor's part. It is only through complete transparency of ego that the actor can truly transform himself into the character in service of the play. When actors do this honestly and believably then the audience gets swept up in the drama and falls into what we call the "suspension of disbelief." They "forget" for a while that they are watching a play step into the mind and emotions of the fiction. This transportation is impossible without the actor's inner sense of truth.

This is why. When an actor thinks of what they are doing as "performing," they have a tendency to place much of their attention on themselves, on *their* "performance." Actors then often feel unduly and irrationally responsible for being "interesting" rather than making the events happen. When actors think of what they do as "living," they are liberated from the burden of having to "give a performance" or be "interesting" and are better able to place all their available attention on their scene partner. This may on the surface seem like splitting semantic hairs. But let's go back to one of our earlier premises that "how you talk about your work is how your work will be." We then realize that in this important selection of the word "living" over "performing" the actor is liberated from "self" and the lower ego. They are free to place all their attention on their scene partner and play action onto them.

 ACTORS DON'T GIVE A PERFORMANCE, THEY GET ONE—FROM THEIR SCENE PARTNER.

Now you can begin to see that the semantic yet important suggestion to "live" believably rather than to "perform" believably helps actors go deeper into the fiction. The ultimate irony is that making "interesting choices" as an actor is like trying to heard cats. They are capricious and finicky littler buggers at best; the harder you try the more they run away. But as soon as you ignore them and fully invest yourself in the other person and the action, it's like you were born full of artistic catnip! The work becomes much more interesting because you are actively doing something worth watching. A multitude of interesting felines then come running to you!

Do you know that in the Balinese language there is no word for art? The reason for that is that they view life itself as art. Now that's really living believably and creatively!

EXERCISE

Answer the following questions:

Have you found that when you are in front of the class you are "performing" or "showing off?" Or, have been able to focus on your scene partner and what you are "doing" in the moment? Use the space below to note a few observations of your in-class performance experiences.

CHAPTER

"All art is improvisation."

- STEPHEN NACHMANOVITCH

SPONTANEITY AND FORM

Acting, like all art, is improvisation within a form. Improvisation requires spontaneity. Spontaneity manifests itself via choices made in the moment, whether by an actor, musician, painter, writer, or other artist. These choices are instantaneous reflections of a composition of intuition, technique, training, rehearsal, and experience. The shape, familiarity, and strength of the form will ultimately dictate the artist's facility to work with this spontaneous expression. The particular form within which actors improvise is determined by a combination of the style or genre of the writing, the given circumstances of the script, the design concept, the other cast members, and the director's vision. These components are the details that give shape and specificity to an actor's portrayal. Without these behavioral and contextual roadmaps, the actor's work would be sloppy, uninformed, and most likely repetitive and/or indulgent. Form can at first feel like a straightjacket to the beginning actor. However, once embraced, it frees the actor's impulses, leading to a more precise, articulate, and deeply creative expression. For example, unless the design concept and directorial vision are of a modern day approach, an actor in one of Shakespeare's 36 plays will not speak, move, nor act like they would were they at home hanging out with their friends watching television! Their professional responsibility as an actor is to shape their behavior to meet the needs to the text, the era in which the play is set, and the overall concept of the show. Once they have done this, then they are free to "play" with each other extemporaneously. The actor must be able to improvise within the parameters set by these determinants otherwise their work will be wooden and lifeless.

As an analogy, think of acting like a tennis match. There are boundaries within which a tennis player must hit the ball; there are rules and regulations regarding how to play the game. All the parities involved, the players, the umpire, and the audience for that matter, agree upon these rules. This is the form. Yet, within those sharply drawn lines, both players improvise and spontaneously react to what they are receiving from the other by hitting the ball back and forth. This is the extemporaneous doing. But they must "do" so within the base and sidelines of the court. Acting is similar. Actors must stay within the boundaries of the form. For each particular production, much of rehearsal is about finding, determining, and agreeing upon where those lines of behavioral form exist. Once found, actors then hit the ball of "action" back and forth much like tennis players do the ball. (Playing Action will be discussed in greater detail a little further on in the book.) Have you ever seen two tennis matches that, shot for shot, were exactly the same? Of course not. Live theatrical performances, although with admittedly less room for extemporaneous behavior than a tennis match, are not dissimilar. No two performances are ever the same. By the laws of physics alone it's impossible! Even if all the actors in a play tried to replicate exactly, move for move, word for word what they did the night before, it wouldn't happen. At best an actor who tries to do exactly what they did in the previous performance is focused on their own performance, and, at worst, they are focused on some idea of what they did in the past. Either way, they are not in the moment of play that is happening this time, right here, right now. They are missing the opportunity "to be born to the moment" on stage, now. This is what professional actors do. They live truthfully under imaginary circumstances with complete spontaneity and precise repeatability. The precise repeatability is the form. The complete spontaneity is the "action" of the moment. To maintain the spontaneity the actor has to remain open to instantaneous and constant minute adjustments in their performance based on what they are receiving from the other members of their cast.

IMPROVISATION IS THE "HOW"

Most beginning acting classes, to one degree or another, deal with the issue of improvisation. They do so for good reason, as any proficient actor is invariably a decent improviser. There are different forms of improvisation so, let's make clear what we mean by this for our work in the theatre. Simply put, to improvise, in its purest sense, means to not plan something. It means working without preparation. This is not what is meant by improvisation in acting. Obviously, actors memorize their lines; they rehearse the movement and more or less follow the same physical and vocal roadmap from performance to performance. As we will discuss more in the chapter on precise repeatability, this is what is called the form. The improvisation that we are referring to has to do with "how" you will do what you do on stage, in other words "how" you play your "action"—how you hit the ball back and forth with your scene partner, to continue with the tennis analogy. And 90 percent of the time this will be determined by what you are getting from your scene partner. It is impossible to predetermine what another actor is going to do and how they are going to do it. So, what actors do is make their scene partner the target of their attention. They let them become the "source" of the action and literally take their cue—for "how" they are going to play their "action"—off of what they are getting from the other. This is improvisation for the actor. To do this the actor must remain open and available. They must let go of any preconceived notions of how they are going to play their action and surrender to the moment. This availability allows intuitive and spontaneous reactions to manifest in the moment, and most importantly for artistic surprises to happen.

IMPROVISATION GROUND RULES

Throughout this class you may be asked by your teacher to participate in different improvisation games. Robert Barton in his book *Acting Onstage and Off* lays down some fundamental and helpful ground rules for how to work with improvisation:

1. Participate without evaluating and explore without judgment.
2. Stay involved until the session ends, which means either the situation has resolved itself or the teacher/coach has called it to an end. Accept side coaching, without breaking your concentration.
3. Play to solve the problem, not to find the clever line or cute ending, which may be untrue to the character.
4. Remove preconceptions or plans and respond only in the moment, spontaneously.
5. Accept whatever another actor brings into the scene as true. If an actor enters an improvisation scene, looks at you and shouts, "Brother!" with open arms, don't answer, "I've never seen you before in my life." All new info is accepted. You are now his brother because he established you are; so, hug him. If a new

actor comes on while you are holding a broom and asks you whether your baby is a boy or a girl, your broom is now indeed your baby. You get to decide the sex! Put another way, always say "yes" during an improvisation and go with it. "Yes" and…

6. Avoid toilet humor and vulgarity. It's immature, predictable, and ultimately not very smart or interesting. Rise above it. You're better than that.

CHAPTER 26

PRECISE REPEATABILITY

*"It is the mark of an educated man
to look for precision in each class of things
just so far as the nature of the subject admits."*

- ARISTOTLE

PRECISE REPEATABILITY

Art demands precision. There is nothing sloppy about art. If you look at the later works of Pablo Picasso, his *Guernica*, for example, as we already have, you will find a lifetime of practice, technique, and precision strategically shattered across his canvases. At first glance his images are seemingly random, chaotic, and incoherent in their composition. At times they can seem disorienting and jumbled. Yet, nothing could be farther from the truth. When closely studied, these later works rise to the level of everlasting masterpieces not only for their rigorous and bold originality but also for their taught and masterful execution. Only after truly owning the skillful repeatability of any technique can an artist forge into unknown areas of limitless expression. Of course, as we've already discussed, the figures in Picasso's *Guernica* are not "realistic." Picasso did not choose to· literally or realistically replicate the massacre in the small Spanish town. He knew that any neophyte could do that. Could he have done that himself? Of course he could have; in fact, Picasso had already drawn and painted many works of precise verisimilitude when we he was starting out. However, what gives this painting its power and uniqueness is that the figures in *Guernica* are more symbolic and metaphoric. They are violent imagistic gestures, more suggestive in nature than real. Consequently, these images leave more room for the viewer's interpretation and imagination. Picasso's quote about the evolution of a painting bears repeating here:

"A PAINTING IS NOT THOUGHT OUT AND SETTLED IN ADVANCE. WHILE IT IS BEING DONE, IT CHANGES AS ONE'S THOUGHTS CHANGE. AND WHEN IT'S FINISHED, IT GOES ON CHANGING, ACCORDING TO THE STATE OF MIND OF WHOEVER IS LOOKING AT IT."

- PABLO PICASSO

The more realistic any piece of art is, the less the viewer's role. The more command any artist has over their technique, the more freedom they have to move away from realism. But they cannot do so until they have truly mastered their fundamental techniques. And this takes practice, and practice, and practice, and even more practice. In fact, it is a practice that never ends because it is a life's work for the artist no matter their chosen form of expression. Michael Chekhov says, "Repetition is the growing power." And what he means by this is that it takes years and years of concentrated and precise repetition of any technique to fully become a master of it. Paradoxically, it takes years of practice to achieve the apparent ease and randomness in Picasso's work. All genuine art is precise, never sloppy, in both execution and intention. The same principle of precision holds true for acting.

Walking onto a stage in front of hundreds of people to portray a fictional human being takes not only healthy amounts of courage, but also amazing exactitude in the execution. Nothing can be left to chance. The actors in a theatrical or filmic production must be capable of repeating precisely what they did either in the previous performance or in the previous "take." This is where actor training becomes essential to the longevity of any actor's career. For many a young actor can produce one or two inspired characterizations. But it is the trained actor that can do so show after show, year after year, decade after decade. This ability to precisely carve out a continual variety of non-repetitive characterizations takes a masterful control of technique, much like Picasso's.

EXERCISE

Answer the following questions:

Exercise TO DO: When acting onstage or in front of a camera it is necessary to repeat a performance from night to night or from take to take. Although each performance is spontaneous and new you still have to precisely repeat the blocking and performance direction. The following is an exercise to be done in private. It will help you better understand the concept of precise repeatability. Time yourself for two minutes doing a task from your daily life: coming home from work, cleaning your room, making a sandwich, etc. After you have timed your two minute "slice of life" task, to go back and repeat exactly what you did the first time for exactly two minutes. This means that you need to be acutely aware of your actions the first time in order to repeat them precisely a second time.

What did you experience going through the motions the second time? Were you aware that you were simply "repeating the actions" mechanically, or did you try to "live the task believably" again even though you knew it was just an exercise?

> *"The truth of passion, the verisimilitude of feeling, placed in the given circumstances; that is what our reason demands of a writer or a dramatic poet."*
>
> - ALEKSANDR PUSHKIN

THE GIVEN CIRCUMSTANCES

The ability of an actor to live truthfully under imaginary circumstances is measured against their ability to bring the *given circumstances* of the play to life. This, simply, is the yardstick by which an actor's ability is judged. Because of this, the given circumstances mean everything to the actor. It would naturally be expected that five different actors cast in the same role from the same production would inevitably play that same part five slightly different ways. Yet, what is that intangible quality in an actor that makes us prefer one performance to another? Fundamentally, it is the individual actor's intuitive, idiosyncratic, and creative *interpretation* of the given circumstances that shape audience satisfaction.

Interpretation is everything in the arts. Artistic expression, in fact, demands a novel and unique way of viewing the world, a fresh way of interpreting it, if you will. What is meant by interpretation in acting is the actor's ability to *incorporate* the given circumstances—what heretofore has only been a bunch of words on a page—to give *body* to a *fiction*. Actors do this via their physique, voice, emotions, desires, passions and, ultimately, imagination. Invariably, an actor with an available, facile, and potent imagination is the one the audience wants to watch.

THE GIVEN CIRCUMSTANCES ARE THE FICTIONAL BEHAVIORAL PARAMETERS DICTATED TO THE ACTORS BY THE AUTHOR. THEY ARE THE DEFINING FEATURES OF ANY DRAMA OR COMEDY. IT IS AN ACTOR'S JOB TO INTERPRET THEM.

Reference your own life. Even though you think of yourself as only one person, we have already established that you play many parts and wear many masks on any given day.

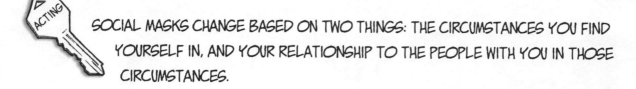 **SOCIAL MASKS CHANGE BASED ON TWO THINGS: THE CIRCUMSTANCES YOU FIND YOURSELF IN, AND YOUR RELATIONSHIP TO THE PEOPLE WITH YOU IN THOSE CIRCUMSTANCES.**

For example, you might be reading this book right now in the library. That is the "*where*" of the given circumstances. Because you are in a library you behave a certain way. But let's say you get thirsty and then leave the library to get a juice at a nearby café. Even if you continue reading at the café, your behavior will shift based on the fact that your "*where*" has changed. We all behave slightly differently in libraries than we do in cafés. Now, let's say some friends come by and invite you to the beach with them. Because you have a "relationship" to these people even though you have work to do, they convince you to finish what you're doing on the more agreeable sand. So, you pack up your stuff a second time and continue reading by the ocean. Once again, *how you do what you do* is shaped by the new *environment* (where), AND the fact that your *friends* are now with you (relationship). Ultimately, your friends distract you to the point that you stop reading, put your book away, and surf the rest of the day with them.

Now, of course, I know that none of you would EVER to this! It is PURELY hypothetical. But I think you get the point.

 WHAT WE DO AND HOW WE DO IT DEPEND ON THE CIRCUMSTANCES WE FIND OURSELVES IN AND THE PEOPLE WITH US.

The same thing is true for characters in a play. Luckily for actors, figuring out the given circumstances of a play is much easier than in life. This is because the given circumstances of the play have been pre-determined by the playwright and are finite in number. Life with its infinite number of circumstantial matrixes is much more difficult to analyze.

 GIVEN CIRCUMSTANCES DETERMINE AND COLOR OUR ACTIONS.

Now, let's take a look at the five questions an actor must answer for themselves to begin to take on any role they wish to play.

EXERCISE

Answer the following questions:

Take a few moments to reflect on your current given circumstances. Where are you right now and how does this environment affect your behavior? Also, consider other factors that may be influencing the way you behave and feel. For example, time of day, public or private, familiar or foreign, people around you, ect.

CHAPTER

THE FIVE QUESTIONS

28

> *"Talent is the ability to live believably under imaginary circumstances. Everything after this is craft and technique. But we need to begin here. This is the thing that we must work. The discipline is what we teach because acting is an art form."*
>
> — EARLE GISTER

TECHNIQUE

Although technique is merely a means to an end and not the goal itself, all good art depends on it. In fact, the word technique is derived from the Greek root *teche* or *tekinos* meaning art. Art demands precision. As we've established, art is not sloppy; nor is art accidental. Technique provides the tools with which the artist can be more precise with their talent. The five questions are the cornerstone of the actor's technique.

"THE TECHNIQUE OF ANY ART IS SOMETIMES APT TO DAMPEN, AS IT WERE, THE SPARK OF INSPIRATION IN A MEDIOCRE ARTIST; BUT THE SAME TECHNIQUE IN THE HANDS OF A MASTER CAN FAN THAT SPARK INTO AN UNQUENCHABLE FLAME."

— JOSEF JASSER

PROCESS

Process for the actor means the work of transformation of self into character, of assimilating all the complexities and nuances from the fiction into their body. It is the means by which actors make the journey into character. Technique provides the actors with tangible repeatable steps and tools by which they can make a potentially ambiguous work specific. Process is the time and manner in which they do it. It is when the actor leaves their everyday self behind and moves to a place of the higher self or higher ego, a place of where creativity ideally transcends the banality of the quotidian and artists work at their highest potential. What acting schools do is take the mystery out of the process and put it into practical, manageable technique that actors can learn and ultimately own for themselves as artists. The vocabulary of technique and its sources allow us to arrive at an artistic common ground in order to talk about process work and understand each other.

Process lies in the ability of the actor to live believably under imaginary circumstances. This is where process counts most. This is what all worthy acting techniques are geared to toward—development of the *imagination*.

THE FIVE QUESTIONS

There are five essential questions that the actor must answer for himself in order to begin processing the part. These questions are a distillation of the revolutionary Russian acting theorist Konstantin Stanislavski's script analysis technique. By answering these questions, the actor begins the process of transformation from self into character. Actors must learn to read a script for its intrinsic acting values not as literature. They must learn to interpret scripts for its merit to them as artists who will breathe life into the characters. These questions provide concrete tools for the actor to facilitate creation and ultimately inspiration.

The professional actor reads their script a minimum of three times uninterrupted before beginning work on the questions. Reading the script a minimum of three times allows the story, the characters, and the given circumstances a chance to "sink in," as it were. After reading the whole story three times, the actor proceeds to work on the five questions.

The five questions are:

1. WHO AM I?

2. WHERE AM I?

3. WHAT DO I NEED?

4. WHAT DO I DO TO GET WHAT I NEED?

5. WHAT DO I DO IF I GET OR DON'T GET WHAT I NEED?

These are the essential questions actors must always ask, explore, and define in order to live truthfully under imaginary circumstances. Let's take them one by one.

QUESTION #1: WHO AM I?

The ever evolving question of "Who am I?" strikes at the heart of every role an actor will play. From the first time they read the script until the closing night performance, an actor works on this question. Actors probe to deepen their understanding of the "Who am I?" They do so continuously as they move from the rehearsal room and out onto the stage.

Actors begin to tackle this monumental question by parsing out the character's *likes and dislikes*. Basically, in life we push things away from us that we don't like and pull things toward us that we do like. We can say then that our *point of view* on the world is shaped by our likes and dislikes. Therefore, it follows that our *objectives* and *actions* are defined and colored by our *likes* and *dislikes*. Hence, the more an actor can identify and incorporate the *likes* and *dislikes* into performance, the closer they will get to the soul of the character. This in turn serves as fuel for the objectives and actions.

THE "WHO AM I?" QUESTION IS PRIMARILY SHAPED BY THE CHARACTER'S LIKES AND DISLIKES.

Depending on the play there can be many more components than just likes and dislikes. But this is a fertile, specific, and active place to begin the creative exploration of character. You can see that by answering these core questions the character immediately begins to take focus. It is the actor's professional responsibility to continuously mine the text for answers to this question until their professional engagement with the role is ended. A composite of questions that comprise Question #1 looks like this:

COMPONENTS OF THE "WHO AM I?" QUESTION:

- WHAT ARE THE CHARACTER'S LIKES AND DISLIKES?
- WHERE WAS THE CHARACTER BORN?
- WHEN WAS THE CHARACTER BORN?
- WHAT RACE IS THE CHARACTER?
- WHAT SOCIAL CLASS IS THE CHARACTER?
- HOW WEALTHY IS THE CHARACTER?
- WHAT IS THE CHARACTER'S JOB?
- WHAT IS THEIR MARITAL STATUS?
- WHAT DO THE OTHER CHARACTERS IN THE PLAY SAY ABOUT THE CHARACTER?
- WHAT DOES THE CHARACTER SAY ABOUT HIMSELF OR HERSELF?

But this elemental Question #1 is not quite as straightforward as it may appear. It is as endlessly complex and multi-layered as you are. It is the actor's job to bring dimension and complexity to the fictional character by using their own human experience, personal sensitivity, and artistic imagination. Finding a precise answer to Question #1 is certainly crucial to the process of refining the whole character—as well as the specific action for that character in any given scene. Question #1 should never be taken for granted due to its seeming simplicity.

Another crucial component of Question #1 inherently involves time. The actor must know "when" they are doing what the script demands of them, because "time" is a huge part in shaping who we are. Imagine if you had been born a thousand years ago, or one hundred, or even fifty years ago, "who you are" would be vastly different than "who you are" now.

PART OF THE "WHO AM I?" THEREFORE INVOLVES "WHAT TIME IS IT?"

COMPONENT PARTS OF TIME:

- CENTURY
- ERA
- YEAR
- SEASON
- MONTH
- WEEK

- DAY
- HOUR
- MINUTE
- MOMENT

QUESTION #2: WHERE AM I?

The "Where am I?" is certainly one of the most important of the five questions. Unfortunately it is the one most often neglected by young actors. It, more than the others, relies on the imagination of the actor to *endow* the space with the requisite fictional environment. In the theatre the "where" may only be suggested by a suggestive or rudimentary scenic design. In film or in television the "where" may be on an actual filmic location. But, as pointed out in the previous chapter, it is the playwright who determines *where* the character is via the given circumstances; and, as we now know, the given circumstances dictate *what* the character does and *how* they do it.

 ENDOWING IS USING THE IMAGINATION TO GIVE FICTIONAL QUALITIES TO PEOPLE, PLACES, OR THINGS THAT THEY DON'T INHERENTLY HAVE.

The actor must endow the space with his or her imagination at all times in all mediums to make the "Where am I?" believable. Question #2 also includes such important factors as whether or not the character is familiar with the location in which the action takes place. Or, in sporting terms, is the scene a "home game" or an "away game" for the character? Or is it neutral territory for all characters involved? Does the scene take place in public or private? Does it unfold in nature or an urban environment? All these components and more create the multi-layered texture of the character's relationship to environment and atmosphere.

 IT IS THE ACTOR'S RESPONSIBILITY TO ENDOW THE SPACE THEY ARE IN—BE IT ON STAGE, ON LOCATION OR, ON A SOUNDSTAGE—WITH THE ATMOSPHERIC AND ENVIRONMENTAL QUALITIES THE PLAYWRIGHT HAS DICTATED VIA THE GIVEN CIRCUMSTANCES.

 COMPONENTS OF THE "WHERE AM I?" INCLUDE:

- ENVIRONMENT
- ATMOSPHERE
- COUNTRY
- REGION
- CITY
- NEIGHBORHOOD
- PLACE

- HOUSE
- ROOM
- FAMILIARITY WITH ENVIRONMENT
- PUBLIC OR PRIVATE
- HOME OR AWAY GAME

QUESTION #3: WHAT DO I NEED?

This question is the character's *objective* in any particular scene. The actor must answer for the character, "What is it that I need, want or desire in this scene?" Normally, there is only one objective per character, per scene. Many inexperienced actors "busy up" the scene by trying to identify multiple objectives. But the better the playwright, the greater the chance that there is only one objective in any given scene. Good actors recognize this as true and keep their objectives clear and strong.

 MOST SCENES ONLY HAVE ONE OBJECTIVE PER CHARACTER.

Once identified, this objective will determine what the character *does* in the scene to obtain its objective. It is preferable, if at all possible, to phrase the objective as a *need* rather than a want or a desire. The reason for this may at first glance seem inconsequential. However, the "Key" from the chapter on *Passion* bears repeating again here:

 HOW WE TALK ABOUT OUR WORK IS HOW OUR WORK WILL BE.

Ergo, the more specific we can be in how we analyze or "speak" about the character, the more detailed we will consequently be in our performance of it. Upon deeper examination we all intuitively agree that things that we *need* are more important to us than those we merely *want* or *desire*. I may *want* a new car or *new* clothes but not really *need* them. But if I am playing a character that desperately needs a car to get out of a life or death situation, or one that truly needs a new suit for an important job interview to keep food on his family's table then the *need* is *vitally important* to me!

 OBJECTIVES MUST BE IMPORTANT AND VITAL TO THE CHARACTER.

"Needs" or objectives live in our guts. In yoga this area is referred to as the lower *Chakra*. The martial arts call it the *Chi* center, which is located in the pelvic region of the body. The successful actor will find a way to "drop" this need into this area of the body. They will literally feel the character's objective as if it were their own. If you really feel the character's need as an actor you are more likely to fight to get it. The actor therefore must find a way to actively and sensitively empathize with the fictional character in order to literally feel its needs.

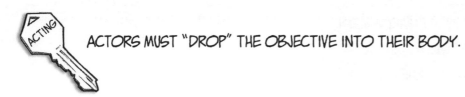

ACTORS MUST "DROP" THE OBJECTIVE INTO THEIR BODY.

How actor's "drop" the objective into their body is beyond the scope of this introductory class. Suffice it to say that the more active the actor's imagination the easier it is. There are a number of exercises at the end of this chapter that will give you some idea of how an actor might go about "dropping in" an objective.

QUESTION #4: WHAT DO I DO TO GET WHAT I NEED?

This question is the character's *action* in the scene. It is the "doing" that we have been talking about throughout the entire book. In the common parlance of actor-speak, Question #4 is known as "playing action."

PLAYING ACTION IS WHAT THE CHARACTER DOES TO OBTAIN ITS OBJECTIVE.

This is such an important component of the actor's process that it warrants its own chapter. We will go into it in more detail at that time. For now memorize the above key to acting.

QUESTION #5: WHAT DO I DO IF I GET OR DON'T GET WHAT I NEED?

This question is two-fold, yet simple. Either the character *does* get what it needs—in which case as soon as the objective is satisfied a new objective comes into play, and therefore a new action to play; or, the character *doesn't* get what it wants, in which case the scene either ends and the same objective picks up in the next scene or the new set of demands of the next scene dictate a new yet related objective.

This question is usually reserved for the odd chance that the playwright resolves a character's objective during the middle of the scene. The puzzlement then becomes for the character, and hence the actor, "What do I do for the rest of the scene if I've achieved my objective?" The answer is straightforward—you have a new objective! And we now well know that if we have a new objective, we have a new corresponding action.

THERE IS ONE AND ONLY ONE CORRESPONDING ACTION FOR EACH OBJECTIVE IN A SCENE; WHAT CHANGES THROUGHOUT THE SCENE IS "HOW" THE CHARACTER GOES ABOUT PLAYING THAT ACTION.

So, let's move onto a deeper exploration of "Playing Action."

EXERCISE

Answer the following questions:

Now that you know the five questions choose a character from a story with which you are familiar. Identify a pivotal moment in the story and answer the five questions for that character in that moment. As you explore, look at the significance that each question has on the character's given circumstances.

CHAPTER
PLAYING ACTION 29

> *"Impulse and passion are the very life-blood of all action."*
>
> - GEORG WILHELM FRIEDRICH HEGEL

PLAYING ACTION

Playing action is the veritable heart of the acting—and impulse and passion are what drive it. I always say to my students that if I was only allowed to teach them one thing it would be this—how to play action. For if you can learn how to play action you have a chance of becoming a professional actor. There is a very simple reason for this:

 PLAYING ACTION PROPELS THE STORY FORWARD!

Actors are storytellers. Their responsibility is to make the events of the story happen in service to the play. We know from previous discussion that where we place our attention is where our energy—consequently our performance—will go. Therefore, to make the action of the story happen, you have to make the other actor(s) on stage the target of your attention and change them in order to achieve your objective. What we actually "do" on stage to change our scene partners is called "playing action." Playing action is the "doing" of the play. If actors aren't playing action then they aren't doing anything to their scene partner. Perhaps they are doing something else. But if they aren't doing unto or onto their scene partner then nothing is happening between them. And if nothing is happening between them then the events of the story aren't happening. And if the events aren't happening, the story isn't being told and the play isn't being serviced. Therefore, an actor who isn't playing action isn't doing their job. It all backs up to this: Actors are doers; they must be playing action at all times in order to make the story happen.

THE DEFINITION OF PLAYING ACTION

The working definition of playing action is:

 PLAYING ACTION IS HOW YOU MAKE THE OTHER ACTOR FEEL.

Advertising executives and fascist dictators have known this for a long time: If you can make a person feel a certain way then you stand a good chance of manipulating, if not outright controlling, their thoughts and actions. Throughout our lives we are endlessly bombarded with commercial images and catchy slogans geared toward changing how we feel about certain consumer products. The advertising industry knows all too well that if they can make you feel desirous of a certain product you will be more like to buy it. Their objective, in acting vocabulary, is to get you to purchase the product they are advertising. For the most part, they are pretty good at it!

Unfortunately for humanity many a fascist leader has also understood this principle. Throughout history innumerable dictators have executed this principle to devastating effect. Events like the holocaust of World War II or the systematic genocides in Somalia and Serbia are seemingly unfathomable to the average citizen. Yet, how do you explain the unthinkable actions of many average citizens in these countries and others? How do you explain the actions of the usually level-headed citizen who under the hypnotic sway of Joseph Stalin of the former USSR, or Pol Pot of the deadly Khmer Rouge in Cambodia, ended up committing unspeakable atrocities? What is it that feeds this normally dormant malignant pluralistic ignorance? How is it that such large groups of normally sane people can come to commit such heinous and insane crimes against humanity? This answer is simple: Their feelings were consciously and actively manipulated by those in power in order to change their thoughts and actions. This goes back as far as Aristotle, and beyond. The art of rhetoric, or persuasive speech, is a potent weapon. Those tragically mesmerizing leaders, and many others, changed how people felt about the acts committed or the subjects of those acts. Once you change how a person feels about something you can more easily change their thoughts and actions.

Examine for a moment your own life. Can you recall a time recently when someone made you feel bad or happy or sad or loved or cared for or stupid or silly? Of course you can. This is what we do all day, every day of our lives! We walk through a never-ending gauntlet of relationships and, therefore, a river of constantly fluid feelings. And with each twist and turn along life's meandering path we are made to feel different ways; we in turn make other people feel things.

 MAKING OTHER PEOPLE FEEL THINGS IS THE NATURAL BYPRODUCT OF HUMAN RELATIONSHIPS.

Actors do the same thing on stage. They analyze their scripts to identify the character's major super-objective and the series of minor objectives throughout the play. Then they choose corresponding actions to play in order to obtain those objectives. When you string them all together and mix them in with all the other characters, you've got yourself a play!

For example, let's say that we have a scene between a young romantic couple, Harry and Sally. From what the playwright tells us, we know that they have been romantically monogamous and living together for the past two years. They both share the common super-objective of wanting to marry and have children. Harry is a lawyer and Sally is a psychiatrist. As this particular scene in the play begins, we discover that it's 5 a.m. and that Harry did not come home last night. Not only that but he neglected to inform Sally where he was or what he was doing. Sally, needless to say, did not sleep for worry and fury; as the scene begins, Harry walks through the door to find Sally sitting up in her pajamas. She is quite angry and says she needs to know exactly where Harry was, what he was doing, and with whom he was doing it. Harry innocently and honestly tells her he spent the night in his office at the law firm where he fell asleep at his desk burning the midnight oil. Of course, Sally doesn't believe him. She thinks Harry is lying and needs Harry to tell her the truth in order to decide whether or not she can marry him. Harry needs to convince Sally that he is telling the truth in order to save the pending marriage. A possible interpretation of these set of given circumstances might be:

- Harry's Objective = Get Sally to believe he is telling the truth.
- Sally's Objective = Get Harry to admit where he really was.
- Harry's Action = Make the actress playing Sally feel = reassured.
- Sally's Action = Make the actor playing Harry feel = guilty.

Now there is a very important dramatic conceit involved in this scenario, one which all actors are aware of, but we haven't addressed yet: the obstacle.

THE OBSTACLE

In any form of drama, be it comedy or tragedy, there is no conflict without an obstacle. If there are no obstacles, there are no actions. No actions, no story. Evidently then every story needs an obstacle to set the characters in motion. The obstacle might be an obvious one like Aliens are attacking planet Earth, or it might be more psychological, like an adolescent's passive-aggressive relationship with their parents. No matter, all stories need an obstacle. Overcoming the obstacle is the primary action of the play or film.

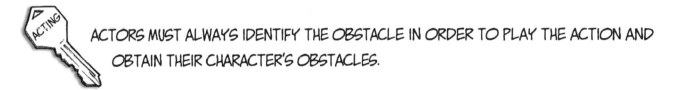 ACTORS MUST ALWAYS IDENTIFY THE OBSTACLE IN ORDER TO PLAY THE ACTION AND OBTAIN THEIR CHARACTER'S OBSTACLES.

Let's go back to our Sally and Harry scene. What's the obstacle there? Can you identify it? Take a few minutes and reflect on the scenario. Then write in the space provided your interpretation of the given circumstances to divine the obstacle in the scene. Talk it over with your teacher to see if you were correct.

EXERCISE

What do you think is the obstacle between Harry and Sally?

PLAYING ACTION IS AN EXCHANGE OF ENERGY

Okay. As we've established, everything we do on stage—or in front of the camera—depends on the other actor. "But how do actors make one another feel something?" you might ask. Good question. The answer is by sending and receiving energy between each other.

 PLAYING ACTION IS AN EXCHANGE OF ENERGY BETWEEN ACTORS.

But what do we mean by energy? Well, in yoga energy is called *Prana*. In martial arts they call it *Chi* or *Ki*. By any name energy is a natural byproduct of living; it is the life force within us all. This may seem slightly suspect to you at this point. So, let me put it into a practical, familiar scenario. Have you ever been sitting across a room from someone to whom you're sexually attracted, when suddenly that person looks right at you and your heart skips a beat, your palms start sweating, and your breath quickens? Well, a "*coup de foudre*," as the French would call it, is an obvious and excellent example of an exchange of energy between two people, or what actors call playing action. To give another example, have you ever been in the act of doing something you shouldn't and suddenly someone catches you doing it? You most likely felt bad, guilty, or at least a little uncomfortable. These are both concrete examples of energy exchanges between people that result in feelings. They are examples of people simultaneously changing each other in the moment.

 PLAYING ACTION IS A PHYSICAL, PALPABLE, TANGIBLE EXCHANGE OF ENERGY BETWEEN PEOPLE.

This is why the earlier chapter on human engagement is so important, because it is the heart of acting, literally. So much of today's world is designed to cut down on human "face time" and quality interaction. I'm sorry, but Myspace, as addictive and fun as it might be, is no substitute for actual human contact! Nor are X-Box games or text messages.

I have another challenge for you. Over the next week I want you to spend an extra second or two *really looking into the eyes* of the people you come across. Just a second or two more than you normally do. That's all it takes. *Really* look at your friends, your classmates, your family, your teachers, the person behind the counter at Starbucks, or the lunch counter. And I mean EVERYONE! REALLY look at them really "take them in." Really "see" them. Do you know what color their eyes are? Are you sure? I guarantee you if you do this for one week consistently it will change not only how you see the people around you but more importantly how you feel about them.

This is what actors mean by "sending and receiving" energy, really taking people in, not just superficially pretending to do so. A good way to start learning how to do it is by making active and engaged eye contact with those around you. Start with those whom you trust and know well. You are undoubtedly familiar with the ancient adage:

 "THE EYES ARE THE WINDOW OF THE SOUL."

Well, there is a very good reason for this: They are! Vision is how we most easily and immediately receive the world around us. Eyesight is also the sense that we most rely on for information about the surroundings in which we operate.

THE "HOW" OF PLAYING ACTION

There are three things that shape "how" actors play action:

1. WHAT YOU ARE GETTING FROM THE OTHER ACTOR(S).
2. THE GIVEN CIRCUMSTANCES OF THE PLAY.
3. THE DIRECTION GIVEN TO YOU BY THE DIRECTOR OF THE PLAY.

These three components shape or give color to the actions actors play on stage. Let's take them one by one.

1. If you recall Tony Barr's definition of what actors do, the first part of it is "*respond to stimuli under imaginary circumstances....*" Ninety percent of the time, the stimulus that actors respond to is their scene partner. What your scene partner does will determine what you do and so on and so forth. Return to our Harry and Sally example. If you are playing Sally and you are attempting to make the actor playing Harry feel guilty then how you play that action will be shaped by the fact that the actor playing Harry is trying to make you feel reassured at the same time! That's the fun and beauty of acting—responding to what you are getting from your scene partner, even if it goes against what you are doing to them. You both change each other simultaneously!

2. How actors play their actions is also colored by the given circumstances dictated by the playwright. In this case, we know that both Sally and Harry are well-educated individuals and work in thoughtful professions. Harry slept poorly at his desk and Sally presumably didn't sleep at all. So they are both unusually tired. These factors, and many others culled from the give circumstances, will also determine "how" the two actors will play their actions in this scene. The given circumstances help flesh out the specifics of how the action will be played.

3. And last, but certainly not least, actions are given shape from the directors of the show. The director of the Harry/Sally scene might tell the actress playing Sally that she wants her to play her action *savagely*, or the actor playing Harry might be directed to play his action *defensively*. Or the director might give them the exact opposite choices. Depending on the director's vision of the scene, the actors can play their actions a multitude of ways.

LOSE YOUR MIND!

Self-consciousness, as we've already established, kills a performance. Now that we know more about what it is actors do, we can more accurately say that self-consciousness is a by-product of self-doubt. If an actor doubts any aspect of their ability, that doubt will act like a black hole and suck all their attention back onto themselves. Ironically, the more the actor's attention goes back on themselves, the more self-doubt has a tendency to increase. This ends up compounding the problem exponentially. In doing so, the action of the play dies a quick and ugly death! If an actor is on stage thinking about any aspect of their performance—their lines, how they look, how they sound, whether they are any good or not, whether they are emotionally connected or not, etc.—while they are performing, they are not playing action. This form of thought is deadly to actors. Often in more advanced acting classes actors will work on a series of exercises designed to get them "out of their heads" and into the "moment." It is advisable that when on stage, the actor "check their brain at stage the door," or at least the controlling, left-side, critical-thinking part of their brain. William Shakespeare, who was an actor himself and wrote for actors, understood the power of thought and how it could force action toward impotency. The following textual extract is from the end of Hamlet's famous "To be, or not to be" speech:

> *"…Thus conscience does make cowards of us all;*
> *And thus the native hue of resolution*
> *Is sicklied o'er with the pale cast of thought;*
> *And enterprises of great pitch and moment,*
> *With this regard, their currents turn awry,*
> *And lose the name of action."*

- WILLIAM SHAKESPEARE, HAMLET

ACT IN THE ZONE!

An athlete who plays a game free of self-consciousness is often said to be "in the zone." The same holds true for the performing artist. The zone is the place of optimum performance and freedom of ability. It is a place of calm confidence where all great artists and champions strive to thrive. Actor training, through a myriad of different techniques, looks to provide the fertile ground for the performing artist to work more consistently in the zone. Zone performances usually happen by chance. But what is chance but luck? We've already stated that luck is when opportunity meets preparation. Training is that preparation.

 LUCK IS NO ACCIDENT.

PLAYING ACTION ONTO AN IMAGE = THE MONOLOGUE

The last thing that needs to be said about playing action is that actors can also play actions onto images. This only happens if and when an actor is left alone on stage and is not talking directly to the audience. A monologue is when the actor is indeed alone as the character, and the character speaks aloud.

 A MONOLOGUE IS A THEATRICAL DEVICE USED BY PLAYWRIGHTS TO SHARE WITH THE AUDIENCE THE CHARACTER'S PRIVATE THOUGHTS AND/OR FEELINGS.

But if the character is alone on stage and not speaking to the audience, then to whom are they speaking? The answer is: They are talking to an image.

Ask yourself the following question: Have you ever been alone and had a conversation with someone who wasn't in the room with you? Have you ever yelled at a person who just pissed you off but who is no longer present? Have you confessed to someone how much you love them when they're not there? Have you given your Oscar acceptance speech in the shower? Or have you ever pretended that you were a sport star winning the game in the final minute of the match while speaking the play by play as you go? Or have you imagined yourself an action hero saving the day just before the world blows up? If so, then you have played action onto images! It's completely natural. We did it all the time as children. It wasn't until we were conditioned otherwise by society and authority figures and told that fantasizing was wrong that we stopped doing what came to us intuitively.

Images are viscerally powerful. You only have to imagine in your mind's eye someone to whom you are sexually attracted to feel how an image can provoke an actual physical response in your body. Go ahead. Try it.

See. You get it now?

I thought so…

CHAPTER
LISTENING 30

*"Stop the words now.
Open the window in the center of
your chest and let the spirits fly in and out."*

- RUMI

LISTENING

At times is seems as if listening is a lost art form. Ever get the feeling that people aren't listening to each other at all, rather just waiting for their turn to talk? They're waiting for the next opportunity to show off how much they know (or think they know), or to prove how smart they are (or think they are), or to impress their captive audience (who might in fact be depressed by all the lower ego talk). The so-called political debate shows currently on television are a perfect example of this. Yet there is no real debate going on because neither side is honestly listening to the other. They are all just waiting their turn to get on the proverbial soapbox and grandstand about what they hold to be true. What is lost in this is thoughtful intellectual exchange between parties. What is lost is the possibility of actual persuasion. Have you experienced any examples of this in your own life? Have you ever been guilty of it as well? I think if we are honest, at one time or another we all have been guilty of not listening. A fabulous teacher of mine once said the following:

"YOU CAN'T LISTEN IF YOU'RE TALKING; AND YOU CAN'T LEARN IF YOU'RE NOT LISTENING. SO, IF YOU LIKE HEARING THE SOUND OF YOUR OWN VOICE, YOU PROBABLY DON'T KNOW THAT MUCH!"

I often wonder about students who talk in class while their professor or a fellow peer holds the floor. Besides being downright rude, these students obviously aren't listening because they are too busy talking, about some weighty topic of worldly import, no doubt. Chances are, while they're yappin' away they aren't learning much either. One assumes that by virtue of the fact that they are in the classroom they are there to learn; they are literally paying money to be there. Right? So, what are they doing? You see the conundrum. It makes you wonder why students like this even bother to show up.

What exactly do we mean by "listening," and what does it technically mean for actors? Listening is more than just receiving information audibly; it is *hearing the true meaning* under the words, which is called the "Subtext." Literally translated, sub-text means, "that which is under the text." We will get into this in more detail in the next chapter. But this is what the actor is listening for, the *truth* that is being communicated in the moment between themselves and their scene partner. And if they are busy performing up a storm in their own little isolated acting bubble then they won't hear very much.

 ACTORS ACTIVELY LISTEN FOR THE TRUTH, THE TRUTH THAT IS BEING COMMUNICATED IN THE MOMENT.

By listening actor's mean making yourself available to your scene partner with your entire body, all your senses, your emotions, thoughts, and soul. At the end of the day what it requires of the actor is to remain open to being *changed* by others. Not only is this important for an actor, it is why they are on stage in the first place! A talented and confident actor deeply *desires* to be changed by their scene partner. They want this because they know this is, paradoxically, the only true way to in turn change their scene partner.

One of my students at Cal State Long Beach, a brilliant young talent by the name of Ms. MacKenzie Meehan, in a moment of epiphany one day in class said it better than I've ever heard it put:

 "OH, I GET IT NOW! THE DEGREE TO WHICH I CAN PLAY ACTION ONTO MY SCENE PARTNER IS DIRECTLY RELATED TO THE DEGREE I MAKE MYSELF AVAILABLE TO THEM!"

Yes! Exactly. Not only did MacKenzie—after two years of learning how to play action mind you—"get it" in that moment, but she took that discovery and went on to gain entrance into arguably one of two top graduate acting programs in the country, New York University's Tisch School of the Arts.

Actors have to be better listeners than the average human being. And by this I mean they have to be more sensitive to all forms of information that is being sent their way: energy, thoughts, emotions, sensations, words, etc.

I'll leave you with one of my favorite quotes by the immortal Yogi Berra:

 "IT WAS IMPOSSIBLE TO GET A CONVERSATION GOING, EVERYBODY WAS TALKING TOO MUCH."

You hear me…?

EXERCISE

Answer the following questions:

Exercise TO DO: Learn to become more aware of when you are not really listening. Once you begin to notice that your attention has wandered during a conversation stop and redirect it onto the person speaking to you. Take this moment to listen more closely to what the other person is really trying to say. Ask yourself what ideas, thoughts, or emotions, are they attempting to communicate? Take a break from your own ideas out and spend one whole day truly listening to the people around.

So after spending some time focused on listening.... What have you learned?

"You cannot play the words. Words do not mean what they mean: We think not that which we say. We say not that which we do. We do not that which we want—And we do it all the time!"

- VIATCHESLAV DOLGACHEV

SUBTEXT

As we mentioned briefly in the chapter on listening, the subtext is that which lies beneath the words. But you might ask, "What could be beneath the words?" Everything!" I would answer you. As per the Russian director and acting teacher Slava Dolgachev's brilliant quote at the top of this chapter, we say things that do not align with what we are thinking all the time. In other words, we say things that we really don't mean. We also do things that we say we're not going to do, and we even do things we say we don't want to do on almost a daily basis. It is part of the delightfully entertaining hypocritical dance known as being human. Very rarely in life, beyond the pedestrian exchange, do the words that come out of our mouths perfectly align with our thoughts, feelings, desires, or actions. In other words the text doesn't always align with the doing. I'm sure you recognize this to be true from your own life.

 SUBTEXT IS THE TRUE MEANING OF WHAT'S GOING ON IN A SCENE. IT THE TRUTH THAT LIES BELOW THE TEXT.

MOTIVATION

Then what this means for the actor is that acting involves the following:

ACTING IS NOT ABOUT MEMORIZING LINES. IT IS ABOUT DISCOVERING WHAT MOTIVATES THOSE LINES.

A common misconception among non-actors is that acting is just about memorizing "all those lines" and practicing how you are going to say them and where you will move on stage. Not so. We've already talked about the three "shapers" of the "how" of action. Do you remember them? (1.The other actor; 2. the given circumstances; 3. the director's vision.) The experienced actor knows that if the preparation and rehearsal processes have been attentive to detail the "how" will ultimately take care of itself in the moment. What an actor in rehearsal does is explore the *motivation* for the lines, not how they are going to deliver them. Everything we do or say in life has some motivation attached to it, even the most mundane of things. Nothing happens in life without a motivation.

 MOTIVATIONS ARE WHAT PROVOKE AND PROPEL THE CHARACTERS INTO ACTION.

What actors actually do, therefore, is mine the text for what *propels* them into action, what we call their motivation. They do this by analyzing the given circumstances. Then actors go out on the stage and play action onto the other actor(s) in accordance with those motivations. Of course they speak the dialogue provided by the playwright. But it is not the words themselves that are important. What is important is what the character means by what they are saying. This, again, is what we call the subtext. It can be said then that the subtext is the real action in the scene.

What this means for the actor is the following:

 PLAYING ACTION IS THE SUBTEXT.

See how it all comes together now?

EXERCISE

Answer the following questions:

Exercise TO DO: Spend one day paying extra attention to the subtext of your conversations. Ask yourself do you really mean what you say? What is the underlying meaning of what others are saying to you? How does this awareness change your conversations if at all?

CHAPTER

"Action is character."

- F. SCOTT FITZGERALD

CHARACTER

Even as far back as 570 BC the Greek philosopher Aristotle weighed in on acting. He stated in his famous tome *The Poetics* that:

"A MAN'S CHARACTER DISPOSES HIM TO ACT IN CERTAIN WAYS, BUT HE ACTUALLY ACTS ONLY IN RESPONSE TO THE CHANGING CIRCUMSTANCES OF HIS LIFE, AND IT IS HIS THOUGHT (OR PERCEPTION) THAT SHOWS HIM WHAT TO SEEK AND WHAT TO AVOID IN EACH SITUATION."

Fundamentally, what Aristotle was saying is that our character works in conjunction with our circumstances to shape our actions. To crudely paraphrase Aristotle's famous *Poetics*, "To be is to do." Sound familiar? It should—character is all about the doing. Ultimately, we are what we do; we are the sum of all our actions. Look at the nomenclature we have for identifying people; we say that someone is an athlete, an actor, a professor, a student, a parent, a police officer, a nurse, etc. We immediately identify people by their occupations. Why is that? One explanation is that we spend most of our lives doing these things; so, it is natural that people associate us with our work. Occupations literally occupy our lives with doing; it makes sense that we become identified as such. This, of course, is just a starting point. People are certainly not just their jobs. But it's an illustrative start. We then break down each character more specifically. Are they a good cop or a bad lawyer? How do we decide? Our conclusions about a person's character are drawn from what we know about *what* and *how* they do what they do. If we parse this out further we will eventually come to a detailed picture of the person we are examining. Their character will soon be revealed through a composite portrait of all the things they do.

"TELL ME WHAT YOU DO, AND I'LL TELL YOU WHO YOU ARE."

— UTA HAGEN

THE MASK OF THE CHARACTER

On some level creating character is why actors are drawn to acting in the first place. Many actors talk of the joy of "losing themselves" in a role. What they mean by this is that by taking on the character they are free to behave in ways they can't in their own personal lives. This is certainly true and one of the sure satisfactions of being an actor. Actors get to live more than just one life! It is certainly liberating to play someone else for a while, to "walk in their shoes" as it were. The mask of the character liberates the actor from his or her own idiosyncratic, personal behavior patterns and habits. They are free to be someone else, or at least act like someone else, if only for a while.

By the term "character mask" we are not referring to a literal mask that the actor pulls over their face, though in some theatre forms like *Commedia Dell'Arte* this is actually the case. What we normally mean by character mask is the fictional semblance of behavior that an actor takes on to tell the story. Actors don't literally wear physical masks (unless they are Freddy Krueger!); the character mask is license to behave differently than they would when they are not on stage. The mask is permission to run wildly into the imagination. The actor is virtually protected by the playwright's creation because actors are required to do what the character does. They are set free to play in the fictional world of the character. The character's mask gives them the permission to play.

The mask of the character invites pure unadulterated play. It beckons us to fantasize like we did when we were children. Remember when in an instant we could become cowboys, Indians, rock stars, cops, robbers, warriors, princesses, kings, generals, doctors, lovers, sport stars, villains, and super-heroes? Why was it so easy then? It was easy because as children our imaginations were limitless and unfettered, that's why! Role-playing is an organic and natural part of being human. Without prompting, children instinctively desire to play other characters and intuitively know how to wear a multitude of fantastical masks. Actor training is geared toward helping us return to that place of imaginative naiveté.

SELF VERSES CHARACTER

However, Uta Hagen in her classic book *Respect for Acting* talks of creating character in a slightly different way:

"I WANT TO FIND MYSELF IN THE PART, NOT LOSE MYSELF."

By this she means that she wants to be able to find parts of herself that closely identify with the character. By approaching the work this way she assures that she will be more inclined to "live" in the role rather than "perform" the role. Tony Barr in his book *Acting for the Camera* concurs with Hagen. He even takes this a step further. Barr suggests that it is best for actors to not even use the word "character" but rather substitute the word "role" when speaking of the part they are playing. Again, an important semantic distinction warrants clarification here.

When actors say that they are playing a "character" they have a tendency to think of the part as something *other* than themselves. It is true they are not literally the part they are playing. Yet, the part is nothing without the actor. The actor will have to find a way of "becoming" the part, or, rather, transforming themselves into the character. Yet, if the word "role" is substituted for "character," Barr postulates that the actor will more closely identify with the part they are playing, and therefore be more likely to "live" rather than "perform" believably. Barr believes the actor's "performance" will somehow be closer to the truth and hence more natural and believable. This is certainly the case for camera work where naturalism is usually the order of the day.

DISTANCE OF COMMUNICATION

What fundamentally separates theatrical performances from cinematic ones is distance of communication. Since in a theatrical performance actors must literally project their performance to the back row of the audience, there is more room for size, or "theatricality," in their creation of character. The size of the theatre literally dictates it. But on film, where the camera lens actually zooms into the actor to "capture" their performance, and then that performance is projected by a machine onto a screen that can be up to three stories high, much more subtlety is required of the actor's work.

QUESTION #1 REVISITED

Without mentioning it, what we have been discussing is question #1 from the five questions. The "Who am I?" is the heart of every character. Incorporating this question into the body and then praxis is what makes acting an art form. Not too many people can do it profoundly and deftly. Many an actor can play a simple action. But "how" that action is played determines the depth of the actor's ability. And part of one of the three "shapers" of action, the given circumstances, is question #1. It can therefore be said that a solid measure of an actor's talent begins with their ability to play action. Eventually though, this is measured by the spectrum of colors they bring in "how" they play that action. The more varied the accompanying circumstances an actor can create, the deeper their talent. The more colors they can bring to their actions, the more specific their characterizations will be.

TRANSFORMATION VERSES PERSONALITY ACTING

Acting is a process of transformation. The actors who play themselves in virtually every role are not very interesting, creative, or talented. They may be a successful movie or television star, but what they are really doing is capitalizing on their own personality and harnessing it in each role they play. Additionally, and more often than not, acting is misrepresented by preconceptions instilled in us by Hollywood and the dreams of fame, fortune, and stardom that accompany it. Let's set things straight. Hollywood is a business; it's about profit. Hollywood stars are vehicles whose main purpose is to sell a product—the film or television show—through their personalities, not their acting ability.

Not all stars are actors, and most actors are certainly not stars. Believe it or not, the one rarely has anything to do with the other. In fact, stardom is an orchestrated accident at best. It is a product of luck. No one can predict who will become a star or why. There is nothing wrong with the business of Hollywood, being a star, or just being plain lucky! We should, however, be clear that one is a business and the other is an art. Occasionally the two overlap, but rarely. Personality actors eventually cannibalize themselves to the point where nothing is left in their work worth watching. That is when the "new flavor" of the month replaces them.

One sure-fire way to avoid this burnout as a personality actor is to never become one! True actors concentrate their energies on the craft of acting and the process of transformation it engenders. The Russian acting genius, Michael Chekhov, said it best:

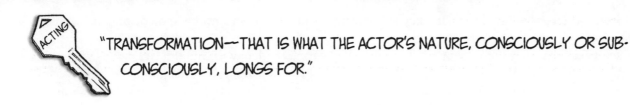

"TRANSFORMATION—THAT IS WHAT THE ACTOR'S NATURE, CONSCIOUSLY OR SUB-CONSCIOUSLY, LONGS FOR."

STARDOM

But if you have your heart set on being a personality actor with hopes of eventually becoming a star, there is nothing inherently wrong with that. Just know that you will have to be very lucky. I have very little to say about luck, other than this:

LUCK IS WHEN PREPARATION MEETS OPPORTUNITY!

In other words, if you're not prepared and don't create opportunities for yourself to be in the right place at the right time, you will never be lucky. So, work hard, always come in prepared, and create opportunities for yourself. Don't count on being lucky.

Make luck happen. Take action. It will be a reflection of your character.

EXERCISE

Answer the following questions:

Exercise TO DO: For this exercise you will need to be in a public place where you have the opportunity to watch a variety of different people. Choose someone who you feel could be an interesting 'character.' Ask yourself, what is it about this person that makes them different or interesting to me. Are you able to get a sense of what they do, who they are and where they're going simply by watching their behavior? If you had to play them (as a character) what aspects of their physicality would you need to embody in yourself? Be aware of how this person is different from you and why.

PART III

THEATRE APPRECIATION

ACTING

CHAPTER

"People are afraid of thoughts. We live in a world of lies. The theatre can change this. And no one who has stood on the side of truth has ever regretted it."

- LEOPOLD SULERZHITSKY

ACTORS AS STORY TELLERS

Hopefully this book has begun to lay bare for you the mystery that is arguably the oldest art form. As long as mankind has been in existence, there have been actors. For long as long as there has been storytelling, someone was needed to actually recount the story. Storytelling is what acting is all about. Actors play different roles to portray a story. Therefore, actors are storytellers. As you have read, to do so successfully actors must shed the social masks they wear in their personal lives, and they must play with the unbridled enthusiasm and imagination of children. Where they do it with the most freedom of expression is the theatre. As far back as Ancient Greece, the first organized theatre that we are aware of in Western civilization, actors were commonly called the Craftsmen of Dionysus, as the son of Semele and Zeus was the patron god of the Greek stage.

The theatre is usually referred to as the actors' medium. Film is the director's medium. Consequently, cinema is considered the field of the person who shapes the overall vision of the film; it is not unusual for the *auteur*, as filmmakers are often referred to, to write the screenplay, and oversee both filming and post production. Television is the writer's medium, for television is mostly about the spoken word. Executive producers on television shows are almost always the head writers. It is they who dictate the form, style, and execution of the show. It all backs up to their writing.

BEHIND THE SCENES

An enormous amount of hard work goes into any theatrical production before an audience ever gets to see it. Of course there are the requisite and expected rehearsals with the actors and directors. But there are also teams of behind the scenes artists and staff who work for weeks, months and sometimes longer on the design and management elements. Depending on the type of theatre and the budget of the production these teams can be made up of only a handful of people or number into the dozens. These talented and often unsung heroes of the theatre act not only as support to the actors on the stage, but also play an essential role in bringing the director's vision to life. Without these vital artists and staff the actors would be left standing naked in silent darkness on a bare stage with no audience to watch them!

THE ARTISTIC DIRECTOR

This person, often times a stage director in their own right, designs the greater artistic vision and aesthetic of the theatre. They oversee play selection, hiring of guest directors, actors and artists. They often act as the public face of the theatre in the community representing the theatre at civic functions and fund raising campaigns. It is their mandate to articulate and execute the theatre's particular "voice" and insure that it stays on artistic course.

THE DIRECTOR

The director is artist responsible for the overall vision of a theatrical production. They rehearse the actors and guide the design teams toward a common vision and act as the unifying center of the piece. Normally, after reading the play a number of times, the director will attempt to find a personal connection with the story that is to be told. In other words they will search for the reason why the script needs to be performed and ask themselves "What relevance does this story have to today's world?" They search for a compelling core reason to do it. It might be because it's a new play that has something important to say to a particular audience. Or possibly it's a classic that has contemporary relevance and immediate resonance. This initial analysis process helps the director identify artistically with the play and will serve as a thematic touchstone to return to throughout the preproduction and rehearsal process. Once they have found their personal connection to the piece the director decides what it is exactly that they want to "say" or "do" with it. This is referred to as the director's vision for the production. By this we mean that the director responds to something in the play and works to bring that thing to fruition. Often they will begin by isolating a theme or image from the story. They then design the show around the articulation of this theme or image. If the play is an original work they might collaborate with the playwright on rewrites of the dialogue or help shape the text into a more coherent, accessible or potent form. If the play is a classic they might decide to set it in a different era or adapt it somehow. This is often done with Shakespeare's plays. Or they might deconstruct the text and present it in a more abstract manner. There are an infinite number of ways to rework a play, limited only by the director's imagination and the logistical capabilities of the theatre. However the director envisions the piece, this "take" on the work propels the entire production team in a common direction toward a common goal. This in conjunction with rehearsing the actors evolves into the director's idiosyncratic vision for the production

THE DESIGN TEAMS

Once the director's vision has been articulated the design teams then go to work. There are a variety of different design units who, in concert with one another, work in specialized areas to realize the director's concept. The director usually begins this process at what is called the initial concept meeting. At this gathering the heads of each design area are present. This is when and where the director presents her or his vision of the production. The heads of each design team then go back to their respective areas and work with their team of artists to begin bringing the director's concept to fruition.

The following is a brief description of the Design Area Heads and their primary responsibilities. Their collective objective is to create the world in which the characters live. These collaborators aim to articulate the theme through function and aesthetic.

Scene designer: this artist is responsible for the design and look of the set's scenic elements. These components include the atmosphere, backdrops, furniture, walls, flooring, sculpture, overall look of the set and any alterations that might need to be made to the theatre's audience configuration. Depending on the show the set might be one static unit that never changes from beginning to end, or it might be a series of ever evolving sets that identify and define the place and time of a particular scene.

Lighting designer: is the artist in charge of lighting the set the scenic designer has created. This involves "painting" the set, as it were, with lights and color to create the mood, time, location and "feel" of the scene.

Costume designer: is the artist who is responsible for creating the look of the clothing that the actors wear. Depending on the production these costumes are often designed and built from scratch or pulled from a costume storage library.

Properties Designer: is the artist who is responsible for all the objects that the actors deal with on the stage and which are not inherently part of the stage set or character's costume. For example, "props" as they are called, can include stage guns, cutlery, cigarettes, watches, stereos, canes, swords, etc. Often props are pulled from storage, built from scratch or found in stores near the theatre.

Sound designer: is the artist responsible for creating the landscape of sound for the production. This can include background sound, sound effects, music and voice-overs.

THE PRODUCTION STAFF

There is also a team of artisans who build and install what the designers have designed:

Technical Director: is the in-house "general contractor" for the theatre. This individual oversees the preproduction, building, installation and removal of all scenic elements.

Production Manager: is the person who oversees the macro-production schedule to insure that all areas deliver their product on time and in conjunction with one another. This job involves maximizing coordination and communication between the separate areas.

Master Carpenters: are the people who build the set designed by the scenic designer.

Master Electricians: are the individuals who rig all electrical needs for the show.

Master Painters: are the people who paint the set, backdrops and props, as needed.

Costume stitchers, Builders and Dyers: are the people in the costume department who actually build, rent, or pull from storage, all the costumes the actors wear.

THE STAGE MANAGER

This indispensable individual is the organizational focal point of any production and the proverbial captain of the ship. These hugely responsible people along with the production manager are the coordination hub of preproduction, and the person who "calls" a show once it is open. During a performance the stage manager sits in a booth offstage, aptly called the Stage Manager's Booth, where they can watch the show without drawing the audience's attention. They follow the progress of the show from their booth and call out the sound, music, light and set cues from beginning to end. Once the show is open the director leaves control of the production in the hands of the stage manager who will steer it until the end of the run; the stage manager gives notes to the actors to insure that the integrity of the director's vision remains intact until closing night.

The Assistant Stage Manager assists the stage manager in a variety of duties as needed and is often a stage manager in training.

THEATRE MANAGEMENT

In addition to the director, designers, production team and stage manager there is another team who toils behind the scenes taking care of the daily running of the theatre. The management department insures that the theatre itself stays organized and financially solvent. In smaller theatres two or three people may wear all these "hats", while bigger institutional theatres have larger staffs numbering into the dozens.

General Manager or Managing Director: this person acts as the Chief Executive Officer of the theatre, overseeing all management and fiduciary teams. It is their job to make sure that the theatre runs smoothly and stays in the black financially.

Box Office Staff: are the people who sell tickets in the box office and deal with phone and Internet ticket orders.

Front of House Staff: is the individual or team who meet and greet the audience as they arrive at the theatre for each performance, answering questions from the public and insuring an overall smooth flow from the front door, box office, concessions to their seats. They act as a liaison between what is going on at the front of the theatre and the stage manager and actors back stage.

Publicity, Marketing and Public Relations staff: this is the team that deals with promoting both the theatre's overall image and the show-by-show publicity for each individual production. This involves traditional radio, television and print advertising campaigns as well as word of mouth, grass roots, thematic and viral marketing plans.

Fund Raising staff: the job of this department is to seek money for the theatre beyond that which is raised by box office sales. In not-for-profit theatres this includes soliciting tax-deductible donations from wealthy individuals, corporate sponsorship and/or state or federal grants. They often also organize fund raising events with special themes to attract new audience members.

Development staff: the mandate of this group is to build a larger subscription or single ticket audience for the theatre's season. They work closely with the public relations, marketing, publicity and fund raising teams to get the word out about a theatre's entire season or single show.

Ushers: are the individuals who hand out the playbills, show patrons to their seats and ask people to kindly turn off their mobile phones! Ushers, like museum docents, are often volunteers of the theatre.

> *"God makes stars.*
> *I just produce them."*
>
> - SAMUEL GOLDWYN

STARDOM VS. ACTING

Additionally, and more often than not, acting is misrepresented by preconceptions instilled in us by Hollywood and the dreams of fame, fortune, and stardom that accompany it. Let's set things straight. Hollywood is a business; it's about profit. Hollywood stars are vehicles whose main purpose is to sell a product, which is the film or television show. Box office revenue is the bottom line. Stars drive opening weekend ticket sales in film and ratings in television; these ratings in turn determine per minute on-air advertising costs for commercials. Yet, not all stars are actors, and most actors are certainly not stars. Believe it or not, the one rarely has anything to do with the other. In fact, stardom is an orchestrated accident at best. No one can predict who will become a star or why. Stardom, like many things in life, is a product of luck. There is nothing wrong with the business of Hollywood, being a star, or just being plain lucky! We should just be clear that one is a business and the other is an art.

LUCK

There is very little to say about luck other than I hope you have a lot of it, and:

 LUCK IS WHEN PREPARATION MEETS OPPORTUNITY.

In other words, if you're not prepared and don't create opportunities for yourself to be in the "right place at the right time," you will never be lucky. So, apply yourself diligently and relentlessly, always come in prepared, and create chances for yourself to show your stuff. To a great extent, how you envision your life is how your life will be as long as you prepare for change and create opportunities for growth—and luck—to happen.

DON'T COUNT ON BEING LUCKY. MAKE LUCK HAPPEN!

STAR QUALITY

Star quality is something intangible yet measurable and certainly recognizable. It is that effervescent "something" that a particular performer possesses. It is the "it factor" that potentially makes or breaks an actor's career. It sometimes is called "presence" or "magnetism." It is the inner energy that draws the audience's eye to one particular actor over another. No matter how one defines it, we are all in agreement that, whether or not we care for a particular star's acting, they have something that radiates in them. Brad Pitt has it in spades; so does Angelina Jolie, as do many other top Hollywood stars. It is an inner glow that shines outward and affects and infects everyone in their vicinity. I believe that we are all born with it; yet, some of us are just more relaxed with sharing that inner light with the outside world than others.

"HE WHOSE FACE GIVES NO LIGHT, SHALL NEVER BECOME A STAR."   - WILLIAM BLAKE

When Dustin Hoffman famously asked Laurence Olivier why he was an actor, Lord Olivier, arguably the best English speaking theatre actor of the twentieth century, replied: "Look at me! Look at me! Look at me!" The more an actor is comfortable with having people watch them, or the more an actor actually craves having people watch them, the easier it is for this inner glow to radiate outward. The more an actor fully accepts who they are, the more they are comfortable in their own skin and the more they are at ease with himself or herself, the greater chance they will have of radiating this inner quality outward. This ease with oneself fills all those around them with ease as well. This is why audiences like to watch one particular actor over another; they sense there is something special about them and are drawn to that. Ease, trust, and confidence are the tools that allow an actor's energy to radiate outward. This radiance, coupled with luck, might possibly lead to stardom. But there's no guarantee…

GLOSSARY

Adler, Stella (1901–1992) - An American actress who for decades was regarded as America's foremost acting teacher. A prominent member of the seminal Group Theatre, Adler was the only American instructed by the founding father of modern actor training Konstantin Stanislavski. Her legacy continues today at the Stella Adler Acting Studios in New York City and Los Angeles.

Aristotle (384–322) - Greek philosopher. Aristotle studied (367–347) under Plato at the Academy and there wrote many dialogues that were praised for their eloquence. He tutored (342–c.339) Alexander the Great at the Macedonian court and in 335 he opened a school in the Lyceum.

Ashbery, John - Poet. Ashbery has won nearly every major American award for his poetry, beginning with the Yale Younger Poets Prize in 1956. Ashbery's works are characterized by a free-flowing, often disjunctive syntax, extensive linguistic play, often infused with considerable humor, and a prosaic, sometimes disarmingly flat or parodic tone. The play of the human mind is the subject of a great many of his poems.

Barr, Tony (1921–1981) - Actor, TV Executive and Teacher of acting. Mr. Barr acted in film and TV during the 1940s and 50s. His book, "Acting for the Camera" is considered one of the best books on the art and craft of film acting he also founded the Film Actor's Workshop.

Beatles - An English Rock 'n' Roll group from Liverpool, who continue to be held in the very highest regard for their artistic achievements, their huge commercial success, and their ground-breaking role in the history of popular music. Consisting of John Lennon (1940–1980), Paul McCartney (1942–), George Harrison (1943–2001) and Ringo Starr (1940–), the group's innovative music and style helped define the 1960s. Their early original material fused elements of early American rock 'n roll, pop, and R&B into a new form of popular Rock 'n Roll and established the prototype for the "self-contained" rock group, breaking the long established stronghold that composers had had with record producers.

Becket, Samuel (1906–1989) - Irish-born playwright who wrote primarily in French, also a novelist, poet, short story writer, screenwriter, and essayist. Beckett is one of the most celebrated and influential dramatists of the twentieth century. Most well known for his play *Waiting for Godot* (1953), with its incongruent plot and seemingly pointless dialogue, his work helped advance the concept of a "Theater of the Absurd."

Berra, Laurence Peter "Yogi" (1925–) A former catcher and manager in Major League Baseball who played almost his entire career for the New York Yankees and was elected (with Sandy Koufax) to the baseball Hall of Fame in 1972. He is one of only four players to be named the Most Valuable Player of the American League three times, and one of only six managers to lead both American and National League teams to the World Series.

Brando, Marlon (1924–2004) - Brando was an Oscar winning American actor who is widely regarded as one of the greatest film actors of the Twentieth Century. He brought the techniques of the Stanislavski System and the American "method" (commonly mistaken for the same acting technique) to prominence in the films *A Streetcar Named Desire* and *On the Waterfront*. He was a student of Stella Adler and Lee Strasberg.

Bono - Song writer and humanitarian. His birth name is Paul Hewson and he is the lead singer of the band U2.

Buddha (approx. 563 BCE – 483 BCE) - Siddhartha Gautama, known as the Buddha, was born in the 6th Century B.C. in what is now modern Nepal. He encouraged people to follow a path of balance rather than extremism. He called this The Middle Way. At the age of thirty-five, he earned the title Buddha, or "Enlightened One".

Chekhov, Michael (1891–1955) - An actor, director, author, and developer of his own acting technique. After studying with Stanislavski in Russia, Chekhov emigrated to the United States and set up his own studio, teaching a physical and imagination based system of acting training. His work established the use of the "Psychological Gesture", a technique in which the actor physicalizes a character's need or internal dynamic in the form of an external gesture.

Declan, Donnellan - British Director. Donnellan was born in England of Irish parents in 1953. He grew up in London and read English and Law at Queens' College, Cambridge. His early work was spotted by a lecturer from the Arts Educational Drama School, who employed him to direct his students. He co-founded Cheek by Jowl theatre company in 1981.

De Vinci, Leonardo (1452–1519) - One of the greatest figures of the Renaissance period. Most well known today for painting the Mona Lisa, but whose talents included sculpture, writing and science. He was considered the ideal "Renaissance man."

Dolgachev, Viatcheslav - He has been a teacher of acting in the most prestigious Russian theatre programs, including the Moscow Art Theatre School. He is currently Artistic Director of the New Theatre of Moscow and teaches at the Actor's Center in NYC.

Dostoyevski, Fyodor (1821–1881) - Russian writer, considered a genius. His most famous book is *Crime and Punishment*.

Edison, Thomas Alva (1847–1931) - An American inventor and businessman who developed many devices which greatly influenced life in the 20th Century. Although some of the inventions credited to him were not completely original, Edison is considered one of the most prolific inventors in history, holding 1,097 U.S. patents in his name, as well as many patents in the United Kingdom, France, and Germany.

Emerson, Ralph Waldo (1803–1882) - Writer, poet, minister Harvard Divinity School. The heart of Emerson's writing was his direct observations in his journals, which he later revised and polished his lectures for his essays and sermons. Asked to sum up his work late in life, he said it was his doctrine of "the infinitude of the private man" that remained central.

Fiske, Minnie Maddern (1865–1932) - American actress, born in New Orleans. Her roles in A Doll's House (1894), and later *Ghosts* and *Hedda Gabler* established Fiske as one of the greatest interpreters of the intellectual drama of her time.

Fitzmaurice, Catherine - Voice, speech, text, and dialogue coach and founder of the Fitzmaurice technique. She has taught voice and text at Yale School of Drama, Harvard/A.R.T., the Juilliard School, NYU's Graduate Acting program, ACT, UCLA, USC, New York's Actors Center, London University, the Central School of

Speech and Drama. She is Professor of Theatre at the University of Delaware, where she teaches acting to undergraduates.

Fitzgerald, Scott F. (1896–1940) - An Irish American Jazz Age novelist and short story writer. He is regarded as one of the greatest American writers of the 20th Century. Fitzgerald was the self-styled spokesman of the "Lost Generation", Americans born in the 1890s who came of age during World War I. He finished four novels, left a fifth unfinished, and wrote dozens of short stories that treat themes of youth, despair, and age.

Friedman, Thomas L. - World-renowned author and journalist, writer for *The New York Times*. A three-time Pulitzer Prize winner, he has traveled hundreds of thousands of miles reporting the Middle East conflict, the end of the cold war, U.S. domestic politics and foreign policy, international economics, and the worldwide impact of the terrorist threat.

Galileo, Galilei (1564–1642) - An Italian physicist, astronomer, astrologer, and philosopher who is closely associated with the scientific revolution. He has been referred to as the "father of modern astronomy", as the "father of modern physics", and as the "father of science". His achievements include improvements to the telescope, a variety of astronomical observations, the first and second laws of motion, and effective support for Copernicanism. In addition, his conflict with the Roman Catholic Church is taken as a major early example of the conflict of authority and freedom of thought, particularly with science, in Western society.

Giovanni, Nikki (1943–) - African American poet, essayist, and lecturer, whose work influenced many throughout the years of the Black American Movement. She now works as a professor in the English department of Virginia Polytechnical.

Gister, Earle - Late 20th Century Master Acting Teacher. Gister is the co-founder of the League of Professional Theatre Training Programs, advisor to the National Endowment for the Arts, and co-chair of the training panel of the Theatre Communications Group, Mr. Gister has played a significant role in the nurturing and development of a large portion of the major training programs in this country. His is the former Associate Dean and Master Teacher of Acting at the Yale School of Drama.

Graham, Martha (1894–1991) - American dancer, choreographer, and teacher is known as one of the foremost pioneers of modern dance. Graham founded her own company, the Martha Graham Dance Company in NYC in1926. Her unique movement style -- widely recognized for its principle of contraction and release -- and imagery reflected the modern art of the times.

Greene, Graham (1904–1991) - English novelist, short-story writer, playwright and journalist, whose novels treat moral issues in the context of political settings. Greene is one of the most widely read novelist of the 20th-century, a superb storyteller. Although a candidate for the Nobel Prize for Literature several times, he never received the award.

Growtowski, Jerzy (1933–1999) - A Polish theatre director and a leading figure of theatrical avant garde of the 20th Century. He was the author of *Towards a Poor Theatre* (1968) and had an important influence on the development of modern theatre.

Hagen, Uta (1919–2004) - A German-born American actress and acting teacher. She taught at HB Studio, a well-known New York City acting school, starting in 1957, and married its co-founder, Herbert Berghof in 1957. She also wrote *Respect for Acting* (1973) and *Challenge for the Actor* (1991), which advocates presentational acting.

Hegel, Georg Wilhelm Friedrich (1770–1831) - Hegel was a nineteenth century philosopher had a profound effect on modern thought. His worked explored the nature of rationality in an attempt to create a single system of thought that would comprehend all knowledge. He also developed the hegelian dialectic, a three-part process for revealing reason that ultimately influenced 19th and 20th Century theories of law, political science, economics, and literature.

Hitler, Adolf (1889–1945) - He was Chancellor of Germany from 1933, and Führer (Leader) of Germany from 1934, until his death. He was leader of the National Socialist German Workers Party (Nationalsozialistische Deutsche Arbeiterpartei or NSDAP), better known as the Nazi Party.

Hussein, Saddam (1937–) - President of Iraq from 1979 until the United States-led invasion of Iraq reached Baghdad on April 9, 2003. As President, Saddam ran an authoritarian government and maintained power through the Iran-Iraq War (1980–1988) and the Gulf War (1991). Captured by U.S. forces on December 13, 2003, Saddam is standing trial charged with crimes against humanity before the Iraq Special Tribunal, established by the Iraqi Interim Government.

Jesus (8–2 BC/BCE - 29–36 AD/CE) - Also known as Jesus of Nazareth, he is the central figure of Christianity. In this context, he is known as Jesus Christ, where "Christ" is a Greek title meaning "Anointed One" which corresponds to the Hebrew term "Messiah".

Lucas, George Walton Jr. (1944–) - American film director, producer, and screenwriter famous for his epic *Star Wars* saga and his Indiana Jones films. He is one of the American film industry's most independent, financially successful directors and producers.

McCarthy, Mary Therese (1912–1989) - American novelist, short story writer, and critic. McCarthy's writing, both fiction and non-fiction, is characterized by a spare, elegant style but also by a caustic wit that earned her both high praise and notoriety. For literary inspiration she drew from her life and from the lives of friends and acquaintances, and she made little effort to disguise her sources.

Meisner, Sanford (1905–1997) - Actor, Teacher of acting. A founding member of the Group Theatre in New York during the 1930s and 1940s, he went on to teach at the Neighborhood Playhouse for more than 50 years. He developed the Meisner Technique of acting, which is still widely taught today.

Monet, Claude (1840–1926) - A French Impressionist painter. Around 1872 he painted *Impression, Sunrise* (*Impression, soleil levant*) depicting a Le Havre landscape. It hung in the first Impressionist exhibition in 1874 and is now displayed in the Musée Marmottan-Monet, Paris. From the painting's title, art critic Louis Leroy coined the term "Impressionism", which he intended to be derogatory.

Morris, Eric –He is the author of 5 best-selling books on acting including, *Being and Doing* and has taught acting to over 20,000 students world wide. The Eric Morris System focuses on allowing the actor to bring to each role the uniqueness of his or her own individual personality and talent.

Mussolini, Benito (1883–1945) - The fascist dictator of Italy from the year 1922 to his overthrow in 1943. Mussolini became a close ally of German dictator Adolf Hitler, whom he influenced. His entry into World War II on the side of Nazi Germany made Italy a target for Allied attacks and ultimately led to his downfall and death.

Nietzsche, Friedrich (1844–1900) - German philologist and philosopher. He produced critiques of contemporary culture, religion, and philosophy centered around a basic question regarding the positive and negative attitudes of various systems of morality toward life.

O'Keeffe, Georgia (1887–1986) - American Painter. Know for painting both abstract, surreal and realistic art. Most noted for paintings done in the New Mexico desert.

Parker, Charles "Bird" (1920–1955) - An African-American jazz saxophonist and composer. Parker is commonly considered one of the greatest jazz musicians and as a founding figure of bebop, Parker's innovative approach to melody, rhythm and harmony have exerted an incalculable influence on jazz.

Pearce, Joseph Chilton - Pearce is the author of many books on human development and the changing needs of children, including *Crack In The Cosmic Egg*, a national best seller, *Magical Child, Evolution's End* and most recently *The Biology of Transcendence*.

Picasso, Pablo (1881–1073) - A Spanish painter and sculptor. One of the most recognized figures in 20th Century art, he is best known as the co-founder, along with Georges Braque, of cubism. Extremely prolific throughout his long lifetime, he produced around 13,500 paintings, 100,000 prints and engravings, 34,000 book illustrations and 300 sculptures.

Plato (428–347 B.C.) - Along with Socrates (469–399 B.C.) and Aristotle (384–322 B.C.), is one of the three ancient Greek thinkers credited with originating Western philosophy. His most famous work is "The Republic."

Presley, Elvis Aaron (1935–1977) - Known simply as Elvis and also called "The King of Rock 'n' Roll" or simply "The King", was an American singer and actor. Presley was the most commercially successful singer of rock and roll, but he also sang ballads, and then moved toward country music. The young Presley became an icon of modern American pop culture.

Pushkin, Aleskandr (1799–1837) - A Russian Romantic author whom many consider the greatest Russian poet and the founder of modern Russian literature. Pushkin pioneered the use of vernacular speech in his poems and plays, creating a style of storytelling—mixing drama, romance, and satire—associated with Russian literature ever since and greatly influencing later Russian writers.

Rūmī?, Mawlānā Jalāl ad-Dīn Muhammad (1207–1273 CE) - A 13th Century Muslim Persian poet, jurist, theologian and teacher of Sufism, known to the world simply as Rumi. His poems have been translated into many of the world's languages and have appeared in various formats. He was also the founder of the Mevlevi order, better known as the "Whirling Dervishes", who believe in performing their worship in the form of dance and music ceremony called the sema.

Shakespeare, William (1564–1616) - English playwright, poet, actor, William Shakespeare authored 36 plays and 150 sonnets and is generally considered the greatest of English writers and one of the most extraordinary creators in human history.

Shaw, Bernard (1856–1950) - Irish playwright and critic. He revolutionized the Victorian stage, then dominated by artificial melodramas, by presenting vigorous dramas of ideas. The lengthy prefaces to Shaw's plays reveal his mastery of English prose.

Socrates (469 B.C. – 399 B.C.) - Greek philosopher. Socrates is revered for his shifting of Greek philosophical thought from the contemplation of the nature of the universe, which occupied the philosophers before him, to the examination of human life and its problems. He was the first to study ethics as a science—that is, to study morality in a systematic, consistent manner.

Spolin, Viola (1906–1994) - Considered as the American Grandmother of Improvisation and is the author of a number of improv texts, her most famous being *Improvisation for the Theatre*. She influenced the first generation of Improv at the Second City in Chicago in the late 50's, as her son, Paul Sills, was one of the co-founders. Spolin developed new games that focused upon creativity, adapting and focusing the concept of play to unlock the individual's capacity for creative self-expression.

Stalin Joseph (1878–1953) - Leader of the Soviet Union from the mid-1920s to his death in 1953 and General Secretary of the Central Committee of the Communist Party of the Soviet Union (1922–1953), a position which had later become that of party leader. Stalin maintained an iron grip on Russia for nearly 35 years.

Stanislavski, Konstantin (1863–1938) - Original name Konstantin Sergeyevich Alekseyev, Russian actor, director, and producer, founder of the Moscow Art Theatre. He is best known for developing the system or theory of acting called the "Stanislavski System."

Strasberg, Lee (1901–1982) - American director, actor, producer, and teacher of acting. He was one of the co-founders of the Group Theatre in 1931, and in 1949, he began a lengthy career at the Actors Studio in New York City. Strasberg is considered to be the patriarch of American "method" acting.

Tracy, Spencer (1900–1967) - Great American actor with more than 78 movies to his credit including *Guess Who's Coming to Dinner*. He won two Academy awards as best actor.

Ueland, Brenda (1891–1985) - Author, feminist. Activist in the women's suffrage movement who served as the first president of the Minnesota League of Women Voters (1919–1920) and as chair of the League's legislative council (1920–1927).

Warhol, Andy (1928–1987) - American artist, writer, director and social figure. With his background and experience in commercial art, Warhol was one of the founders of the Pop Art movement in the United States in the 1950s.

Whitman, Walt (1819–1892) - Widely considered to be the greatest and most influential poet the United States has ever produced. Most famous poem, *Leaves of Grass*.

Wilde, Oscar (1854–1900) - One of the most successful playwrights of late Victorian London, and one of the greatest celebrities of his day, known for his barbed and clever wit, he suffered a dramatic downfall and was imprisoned after being convicted in a famous trial for gross indecency (homosexual acts).

Wilson, Robert (1941–) - Dramatist, theatre director, artist and designer who fuses sound, image, text and movement to create extraordinarily evocative stage sets, exhibitions and installations. He is a leading figure in post-modern theatre since the 1960s.